PRAGMATIC PROGRESSIVISM

AN APPLIED TEACHING PHILOSOPHY THAT PROMOTES JUSTICE AND CHANGE

ANGELA DYE, PH.D.

ISBN: 978-1-959347-18-7

This book is dedicated to my mother.

Shoes, leather pants and t-shirts.

As the first pragmatic progressive, she'll understand.

For the reader, it is how I learned empowerment as voice, choice and dominion.

She'll understand that as well.

Thank you mama.

.

For laboring, learning and leading.

For Life, love, and logic.

For light.

Loving you dearly and endlessly!

CONTENTS

1

HOW IT BEGAN

For me, high school was sterile. It was irrelevant and quite disconnected to my daily reality. I had gone from having a dad at home, to no dad at home, to a new man at home who did not want the job of being dad. There is more that I can say in that my formative brain development occurred in the context of domestic violence and other forms of trauma. However, I think the father/fatherlessness carousel is enough to provide an overview of the voids I experienced as a child... to explain why high school was a season of trouble... and to explain why I needed schooling to be more than about college and career readiness. I needed it to also be about empowerment.

While my habits as a high school learner mirrored the habits of what has been identified today as the "at-risk" student, I still managed to graduate. Even though schooling was dark, my family had ways to make sure I crawled into the light. A major influence was my grandmother's *Wall of Fame* where all seven of her children's high school graduation pictures still hang. I knew my picture was expected on that wall and I was not, especially as the first grandchild, going to be the person to break the tradition. So even though the world was dark, I did a lot of negotiating and navigating through what I have now framed the schooling game. It was that game, influenced by the *Wall of Fame,* that pulled me through and helped me to graduate on time.

After high school, it did not take long for me to realize that the jobs available to me with just a high school diploma were not going to honor my true potential. After taking a year off (which was more about interest—or lack thereof—than it was about strategy), I returned to school. It was a local community/technical college and there I fell in love with learning. Learning in that space was not about schooling as much as it was about relevance and control. In deciding my schedule, my course of study, and my purpose as a learner, I used schooling to transcend my lived reality. It was there, through a new context for schooling, that I began to live a mission-driven life.

From this experience, I decided to pursue a bachelor's degree as opposed to an associate's. I transferred to a small, all women's college who prided itself on being performance-based, student-centered, and abilities-driven

—methods I eventually came to understand as progressivism. Through these methods, the instructional power structure was more flat and horizontal. As a result, I was able to take ownership of my learning and walk into my ideals on individual achievement. In this progressive space, I not only discovered that learning was empowering, but I also discovered myself as a learner along with how to actually learn. In the end, I mastered how to increase my personal power!

After four (plus) years, I graduated with a social science degree (and a teaching certificate) and eventually made my way into the classroom as a teacher. There, I brought with me my personal story and the progressive ideals of my teacher training. I placed students at the center of their learning, and I gave them control and autonomy in the learning process. I found alternative ways for them to demonstrate knowing, and regardless of their reading level, their writing skills, or their behaviors, I engaged them in higher-order taxonomies (beyond the extra-credit questions that come at the end of worksheets). As I grew, I increasingly found ways to make learning standards and textbook readings relevant to students' personal lives. I integrated performance-based projects into my instruction so that studying about effective citizenship translated into living-out effective citizenship. Progressive-based teaching was not just an intellectual decision. In terms of what it had done for me, bringing me out of my own demise and personal darkness, it was a moral one.

Through a more progressive model, the line from the spiritual song "Amazing Grace" has meaning... *I once was lost, but now I am found.* Personally, I could instinctively relate to students in the darkness. However, through instruction (as guided by a progressive model), I was able to relate to them in the light!

MOVING BEYOND PROGRESSIVISM

My experiences as a high school student and then as a college student gave me a personal understanding of the benefits of a progressive learning model. But if I am honest, being a progressive educator worked only because I was willing to reach outside of the progressive box and locate and use other methods that would generate results in which I could be proud.

While I will offer ideals and strategies throughout this book for transitioning into pragmatic-progressivism (my approach for extending beyond the progressive box), I want to dedicate the rest of this chapter to three powerful educators who helped me gain clarity and confidence as I made the transition.

LISA DELPIT

Having approximately twelve years of post-secondary education, I have been exposed to many books about teaching and learning and I am proud to admit that many have had a transforming impact on my practice. However, when I read *Other People's Children: Cultural Conflict in the Classroom* (Delpit, 1995), I was moved in a way that no other text had moved me as a classroom teacher.

I was fortunate to start my teaching career in progressive spaces... in spaces that promoted group work, collaboration, authentic assessments, and performance standards and abilities. While these environments allowed me to thrive in my progressive philosophy, I often found myself in conflict with my colleagues. I once was called to the office when my principal discovered that I required one of my students to participate in a weekly reading-writing activity. As I recall, she was very concerned that this particular 6th grader, testing at a 2nd grade reading level, was being required to read news articles and write one-paragraph responses. Besides, as she reasoned, the student wanted to be a limousine driver when he grew up and did not really need to know how to read and analyze text. On another occasion, in a different school, I faced tensions with my colleagues when they discovered that I ordered desks and opted away from the school's use of tables to seat the students. What they later discovered, but could not originally imagine, was that I still used group work as a central means of instruction. But, with the desks, I could set stronger parameters on the process of learning so that group work was more productive. Finally, on yet another occasion—at the same school, I was questioned on my high expectations. First, I was questioned why I assigned homework almost nightly and whether homework was necessary for learning. I was later challenged on my annual ethnography project and was told that this level of work should be experienced in college—not in high school.

Although I was fairly new to my craft, my training as a social scientist created a conviction within about sociopolitical mandates for disenfranchised learners that progressivism did not address. Therefore, I withstood most of these criticisms as a crack in our moral purpose for teaching and continued on with infusing traditional strategies alongside of my orientation for a progressive pedagogy. But I never understood the toll that being politically disjointed from my peers had on me—particularly in that we were so in sync with our commitment to progressive ideals yet so disconnected from political justice. That was until I got a hold of Delpit's book.

As I read her text and heard about her own challenges, quite similar to mine, I began to understand why I was not as progressive as my colleagues **and** why my *altered-progressivism* was perceived to be a problem. It was there, in what could probably be the first educator book that I independently purchased for myself, that I finally understood who I was as a teacher. After years of sitting in teacher lounges or in school-wide meetings feeling fairly disconnected, I finally got it. According to Delpit, there are methods within a progressive practice that only help learners who are advantaged yet hinder those who are not. Being a teacher committed to the success and achievement of all students, it simply was not enough for me to engage in a practice that generated strong results only for some and not for others.

I am forever indebted to Delpit and am so glad that I was finally able to meet her. Not only did she help me to be okay with some of the more traditional/conservative tenets of my practice, she gave me permission to hold onto and celebrate the progressive ones as well! Through her writing, it was okay for me the progressive to embrace the side of me that was more pragmatic.

MARVA COLLINS

Once I learned the value of traditional methodologies, I wanted more. I was not really interested in throwing progressivism away; I was just interested in learning more about other methods. Truthfully, I was challenged to see if I had it in me to be a strong traditional teacher as much as I was a strong nontraditional teacher. I had read a book written by Marva Collins, who was clearly more traditional (classical) in her teaching than I was in mine, and I felt taunted. Collins made a strong argument for tradition in the academic success of Black children. In my charge to successfully serve Black students (as well as other students located at the margins), I was intrigued by the possibility of becoming even more traditional. In short, I wondered if I could do it. I eventually gave into the challenge and went to teach in one of her schools (or a school that operated under her name, philosophy, and training).

I learned a lot about traditional style instruction (as it was the first time I was truly in an environment that promoted it). I learned about what works with that approach to teaching and why it works. I learned about the need to equip low-income and racially disadvantaged learners with literacies associated with schooling—and not just equip them with literacies for learning. (This shift in thinking was radical in that I had been trained to believe it was wrong to teach students for schooling.) I learned about the classics in literature, philosophy, and the arts. I learned about classroom control and how to create a climate of scholarship. Finally, I learned about the power of language and how to leverage it. While Delpit taught me that it was okay to embrace a more pragmatic side to my practice, Collins taught me how to do it... and how to do it well!

I did not stay long at her school. Once I conquered what was there for me to learn, I left. And like with Delpit, I also had an opportunity to engage in a one-on-one, direct conversation with Collins. You see, years after I had left her school, I called her number (or some number left for the public). While I did not know if I would truly reach her, I still left a message. It did not take long for her to call me back. We talked for an hour not just about the instruction of Black children but on the politics of schooling as well.

By the time of this call, I was running my own school (one that I had founded) and was so in need of a deeper understanding of the politics I was experiencing. So beyond teaching me about the advantages of traditional strategies with disadvantaged learners, Collins also helped me to better understand the politics of schooling. While I learned at her school the value of teaching students for schooling, she, in that call, ultimately challenged me not to succumb to it. As a result, I hung up the phone existentially knowing that my work was about confronting the politics. It was about the movement, transformation, and liberation of students who have been pushed to the margins of society. In that one call, I learned about why I needed to be a leader of deep change —about why just being a school leader was not enough! She inspired me to more fully embrace what I already knew. I was a social change agent. Social change agentry (not traditionalism or progressivism) is what should always drive my work with students!

GLORIA LADSON-BILLINGS

While I have always had a personal interest in the success of Black students, I have had a greater interest in the success of low-income students. Therefore, in the first half of my career where I served Black, Brown, Indigenous, Asian and White students living in poverty, I did not have the space to delve into the unique needs of Black students in poverty. It is true that Marva Collins gave special attention to the teaching of Black students and she may have even raised the awareness about the needs of students living in poverty but she never delved into the politics of being Black while also being poor. This intersection of race and class and its impact on the teaching and learning process is what I learned through Gloria Ladson-Billings.

I encountered Ladson-Billings, the researcher behind *culturally relevant teaching*, through my doctoral studies. Not only did her work reinforce my values about instructional relevance, community context, and teacher resistance, it also taught me how intersectionality was impacted by the concept of Whiteness—in how the social elite secures power by way of institutional controls such as education and schooling. Through Ladson-Billings, I learned the politics of education (not just schooling) and how it is positioned to reinforce current distributions of power.

In that Delpit made me aware that Black students need access to traditional teaching methods (alongside progressivism) and Collins taught me actually how to do the traditional, Ladson-Billings taught me that the entire system is about preserving pre-established structures of power. Through it all, the lines between progressivism and traditionalism are no longer as pronounced as they once were. I now (with the help of additional research from John Gaventa) look at all methods of education as relating to power and how my commitment to student and community empowerment needs these methods purely to help students build power, share power, and even resist (oppressive) power. In whatever methodologies I use to work with students and their families, I must always identify the location and flow of power and I must always consider how that power not only empowers but how it disrupts the power structures that promote oppression.

THE FRAMING OF THE PRAGMATIC PROGRESSIVE

Throughout my career, I have come to identify as not just an educator; I identify as an effective one. Unlike most progressives, words like *achievement, results,* and *outcomes* do not scare me. In fact, they drive me. And for this reason, I cannot be married to progressivism simply because of its ideals. I use progressive teaching strategies to achieve results and when they are not effective, I am compelled to try traditional strategies (such as behaviorism, idealism, and realism) as well. Being that my aim as a teacher is to be effective (as well as being liberatory and disruptive), I am under the charge to teach by any means necessary (legally of course). As a result, I see myself as a progressive educator with the willingness and ability to differentiate my instruction to include tenets of traditionalism. For this reason, I ultimately call myself a pragmatic-progressive educator. I hope that the story I shared above about my evolution will give other educators a desire for a more blended model—reconciling progressivism and traditionalism (in the strengths that they both offer).

PRAGMATIC PROGRESSIVISM DEFINED

As already stated, I was trained as a progressive educator. In my training, I was taught that students should be at the center of learning (Parker Palmer). I was taught that schools should prepare students to live and engage successfully in a democratic environment (John Dewey). And, I was taught that higher-order thinking includes reflective and subtle thinking and that learning void of metacognition hardly, if ever, transcends or transfers to novel and complex action (Alverno College). Through these tenets, I started my teaching career with a fairly progressive paradigm. Over twenty years later, I still hold these instructional ideals to be true. While at the same time, I have come to learn and accept that these ideals alone do not successfully serve all students.

Progressive educators with the best intentions are losing the opportunity to have a major impact on the climate of today's education. Today's climate focuses on achievement, accountability, and measurable growth with many progressives shunning these outcomes—insisting that whole child development cannot be reduced to the trivial data that drive these agendas. While education reformers have unjustly reduced whole child development to a data-generating contest, the real problem is that progressives (champions of long-term storage and transfer, sociopolitical liberation, psychological and emotional well-being) do not understand the political demands placed on education by the public—an entity that not only allows for the data factory model but who almost demands it. Although there is a reasonable argument against such a public treatment of education, progressive educators must embrace that education is about the world in which the learner resides as much as it is about the learner himself. As a result, education must also be about community, particularly when serving individuals facing collective hardship. (This point will be discussed more in the final chapter.) Focusing solely on the child may seem morally upright, but it is my argument that it ultimately makes progressives politically irresponsible.

Like the progressive, the pragmatic progressive is an advocate for the humanity of each child at the individual level—promoting freedom, equity, and justice—while at the same time it is committed to the advancement of the collective—the communities in which the children live as well as the country as a whole. The pragmatic progressive holds both of these considerations (the individual and the world) in high regard and does not see a conflict in this dual pursuit.

Admittedly, it is not an easy undertaking to employ this dual pursuit (which inherently is counterintuitive), and there are necessary tradeoffs when trying to do so; however, when properly framed and implemented, the either-or illusion embraced by progressives and traditionalists is, for the pragmatic progressive, dispelled. In economic theory, desired outcomes come at the hands of an opportunity cost and one's willingness to engage in the tradeoff. Such is the case with the pragmatic progressive. Instead of choosing between two distinct methodologies (and the types of learning they each offer), the pragmatic progressive sees the bigger picture. He understands that they each offer a type of learning necessary for living in the social world as it currently is and as it could be. As a result, the pragmatic progressive engages in a tradeoff, securing a win-win for the advancement of the individual and the advancement of the collective.

It is important to note that this dual pursuit of being committed to the individual and the world of the individual does require a merging of two philosophies—and therefore methodologies. However, instead of traditionalism embracing tenets of progressivism (as represented in today's schools), this dual pursuit only works if progressivism embraces tenets of traditionalism—giving it more centrality and weight. Also, as I will discuss at the very end of this book, progressives should be willing to acknowledge pragmatic progressivism as a prescription **and** be willing, at the same time, to toss it out. The dual pursuit of two philosophies is not about what they *look like* in an emerged state but about what they *accomplish* when they are in fact merged. Pragmatic progressivism is about results more so than it is about a philosophy. While I will take great care in other chapters to roll out the philosophical and tactical tenets of the practice, I want you to understand and accept that being a pragmatic progressive is ultimately about impact and change.

The Purpose of the Book

The purpose of this book is to describe the necessary link between progressivism and traditionalism and to offer suggestions for the emerging practitioner to move forward as a pragmatic progressive (where the progressive embraces tenets of traditionalism for the successful advancement of all children). Before moving forward, however, it is important to make a critical distinction. Theoretically, pragmatic progressivism is not directly aligned to progressivism and traditionalism, or even pragmatism for that matter. In terms of learning theory, it is aligned to constructivism, social reconstructionism, and behaviorism with cognitivism operating as the link between them all.

Later in the book, I will talk more about the learning theories behind the practice but in this introduction, it is important to point out the politics of the pragmatic progressive. The pragmatic progressive understands that politically, the school has a function. So, instead of bypassing this function, the pragmatic progressive embraces it. He uses schooling to advance the individual and the collective.

America's schools are currently being impacted by several key forces. First, there is the browning of our country and therefore a browning of our student body. According to National Public Radio (2017), the population growth among Whites is slowing down while the population growth among communities of color is increasing. It is believed that students of color make up the majority of the student body and that by 2044, there will not be a racial majority within the general population. Not only does this shift upend voting traditions that have been accepted, it also changes what it means to be American. As a result, it changes what it means to provide education in the public schools of America.

Next, there is a persistence of an achievement gap produced by a change in student demographics all in tandem with the maintenance of White, patriarchy-capitalism. This persistence, particularly among political progressives, has demanded reconciliation; however, up until this point, such reconciliation has been located in equity work that is mostly assigned to teachers at the classroom level. The unfortunate consequence with this construction of work (in both how the problem is defined and then how solutions are constructed and implemented) is that it does very little to address relational position between affluent-White students and their counterparts. The stratified nature of power throughout history shows White students achieving superior outcomes and this is all due to systems that are designed to produce such superiority.

Finally, there is a movement to vilify any recognition of education as a political agenda (that develops, promotes, and protects one group over another) as well as recognizing Whites (by way of Whiteness) as the racial elite. While critical race theory is not a theory used to engage K12 learners, it is being currently used as the smoke screen of protecting the status quo. Anything that challenges traditional interpretations on what knowing is, who the knower has been, and what knowing is intended currently is being deemed to be racist.

With these three forces influencing how we currently experience school, a teaching philosophy (and practice) is needed that will disrupt traditional stratifications and imagines teaching and learning beyond the standard of White superiority. A teaching philosophy and practice, much like pragmatic progressivism, is needed to ensure all students, even affluent White students, achieve within and beyond their political context so that America's principles of life, liberty, and the pursuit of happiness are those experienced by every American (and not just the racial elite).

The pragmatic progressive in many ways is described by Ladson-Billings as culturally relevant education. She will be discussed at greater length later in the book but this introduction draws attention to her research as profiled in *The Dreamkeepers: Successful Teachers of African American Children* (2009), where she argued that culturally relevant teachers use a number of methodologies, come to the classroom willing to learn from and with their students, and see knowing and being as politically fluid as opposed to being politically fixed. She does not use the phrase pragmatic progressive, but she profiles teachers who embrace a pedagogical range. It is this pedagogical range that is at the heart of the pragmatic progressive that challenges some of the essential methods favored by progressives.

If not already noticed, this book will challenge the constructivist more than it will challenge the behaviorist... it will challenge the left more than it will challenge the right... it will challenge the progressive more than it will challenge the pragmatist. That is because the pragmatic progressive is more progressive than pragmatic. This book has actually been written for the progressive—

to help him strengthen his game so that he can actually produce and promote a progressive agenda in a climate being swallowed by a conservative mission.

The Remainder of the Book

There are two writing styles offered in this book: a personal narrative (mainly captured in the first and fifth chapters) and an academic persuasion (offered in the middle chapters). I started off wanting to be free from the historical underpinnings of the practice. I wanted to share my personal story in how I arrived at the pragmatic progressive designation and show, through my experiences as a disconnected student and my learning curve as a progressive educator, why progressive education is necessary—and why it is not enough.

In Chapter Two, necessary changes for progressive education are offered so the practitioner can walk successfully into pragmatic progressivism. In Chapter Three, I will provide practical tactics necessary for the implementation of the pragmatic progressive along with some theoretical support for such tactics. In Chapter Four, I talk about the philosophical poles of pragmatic progressivism and how together they can break or make the practice. In Chapter Five, I provide a personal update on how I am now living out my work as a pragmatic progressive. I end the book with a letter to the emerging pragmatic progressive so as to be clear and steadfast on the necessary journey of pragmatic progressivism.

Before moving on, I want to talk directly to the sensibilities of the reader. You are not being asked to keep an open mind. You had an open mind when you picked up this book to read it. Instead, you are being asked to be acutely aware of your own beliefs and your own resistance to what is being offered; and, as a result, your own readiness for whatever seems appealing. Sit with it. Consider it. And move forward however you can. The pragmatic progressive is a living and breathing process. It is my desire that through this reading, you will be strengthened in the journey.

2
POLITICAL SHIFTS OF THE PRAGMATIC PROGRESSIVE

The pragmatic progressive, just like the progressive (its sister), believes in the freedom, personhood, and creativity of all individuals. And the pragmatic progressive, just like the progressive, recognizes the collective needs of the human experience right alongside of the needs of the individual. In contrast with essentialists (our colleagues with a more conservative orientation), pragmatic progressives (just like progressives) regard the political and social context as critical to the promotion and protection of freedom, personhood, and creativity for all—for the individual and the collective. In short, collectives matter to the pragmatic progressive (and the progressive)—and the context of the collectives matter as well!

But, there is a difference between the pragmatic progressive and the progressive. Pragmatic progressives not only recognize the collective in terms of their students but they feel instructionally accountable to them. While progressives recognize the collective and want to protect students as collectives, they instructionally respond to them as individuals. And for the learning process, this individualism certainly is vital; however, for the collective as a whole, this individualism is not enough. For many communities at the margins, they have historically been afforded a different grade of schooling. At the same time, they have been deemed as objects (not subjects). As a result, they are cut off as agents of knowing. While the schooling and sociopolitical experiences of those at the margins are two separate conditions, it is important to remember them as interrelated. Thereby, how we educate the collective (while in tandem with the individual) must have its own distinct recognition.

In order to capitalize on the ideals of freedom, personhood, and creativity championed through progressive education, progressives need to embrace four important acts necessary for the collective: isolation (as in skills and concepts), testing, reporting, and accountability. While these events might already be in place, they are often mandated and progressives, therefore, do them begrudgingly (if at all). To really honor the collective (as we do individuals), we must also be responsive to the collective (as we should be to individuals). In order to engage responsively (and responsibly) as educators, isolation, testing, reporting, and accountability must not be acts in which we comply. They must be acts in which we control.

Pragmatic progressives willingly embrace skill isolation, testing, reporting, and measuring and as key events for protecting and promoting the freedom, personhood, and creativity for the collective in which our individual students belong. As a result, they see the shift as more political than tactical (going from reactive to proactive) and work hard to position themselves at the control station where these events are decided.

ISOLATING

During my doctoral research, I discovered a need to carve out a specific scope for student power. I went into the dissertation seeking to explore ways students of successful teachers were empowered. However, I noticed a gap almost immediately as relating to power. In the midst of classroom methods that could arguably be identified as best practices, I found it difficult to see students as liberated, free, and creative agents.

Interestingly, I entered the dissertation with an *empowerment framework* (Dye, 2012). I had assumed the framework, in the way it was constructed, would help me identify student power in action. Instead, I discovered that my framework for empowerment never defined basic foundations to student power, thereby making it impossible to locate it in practice. As a result, I concluded that best practices are not best for students if they do not position them as subjects (i.e., agents) of power.

The pragmatic progressives' emphasis on skill isolation is located at the heart of student power at the most basic level. It is a political commitment to position students as agents of power and to position learning as a utility of power. With this focus in mind, learning objectives become tools of power but only if skills are isolated so that they can be manipulated, transferred, and applied for impact and transformation. Skills and concepts are isolated so that they are available as objects for agency.

Student power is about giving students agency **to do**; and, therefore, the tool (the object of power that students use) makes the agency real. The power tool moves student power from being abstract to it being quite tangible. Isolating skills, and framing them in clear, concise, and measurable objectives, turns learning into an act of accessing and engaging in power. As a result, the pragmatic progressive embraces learning objectives that isolate skills and concepts (along with making them relevant and functional with students' agency).

It is important to note that skill and concept isolation is not only important for power but it is also important for learning. In order for the learner to retrieve what he has learned, what was actually learned has to be retrievable. Often, progressives focus on the application of skills but fail to consider the selection process of the skills that are to be applied. When we carve out skills and concepts as distinct units of learning, they can be identified, evaluated, and then selected in the act of application.

MEASURING

Measurement is another area that doesn't receive fanfare from progressives. In the current climate of over-testing and its toxic impact on student learning and achievement, measurement is viewed as antithetical to the progressive agenda. In that the progressive agenda is worthy, it stands to reason that we should measure its impact and not get sucker-punched by a one-sided conception of tests.

"Inspect what you expect" is a saying I have grown to appreciate. In short, it centers measurement as the means in which expectations are realized. If whole child development, liberation, and creativity are expectations held by progressives, why wouldn't we want to measure the progress made towards these ends?

It is true that standardized tests measure limited skills. Equally true is the premise that progressives are champions of skills that exist beyond the scope of standardized tests (such as leadership, citizenship, and innovation). Because, however, these skills cannot be effectively captured by standardized tests, they are often not measured. By inspecting what we expect, progressives must show a serious commitment to these skills.

Through measurement, these skills are presented as concrete (not abstract) and are able to be pursued and captured with intention.

The pragmatic progressive gets the commitment. Along with traditional skills measured by standardized tests, pragmatic progressives will concretize skills related to wholeness, creativity, and liberation (framed as liberatory skills) and are determined to measure them equally. By turning liberatory skills into tactical measurable outcomes, pragmatic progressives find creative ways to inspect what we do, in fact, expect.

REPORTING

In the previous section, standardized tests were positioned as antithetical to the progressive agenda. In contrast, standardized tests were accepted within the pragmatic progressive agenda. This difference in how progressives and pragmatic progressives relate to standardized tests is political more than it is educational and it could be argued that it is the essential divide between the two groups.

While pragmatic progressivism is tied to the progressive agenda, it has (as stated at the beginning of the chapter) a different relationship to the collective. Both groups, progressives and pragmatic progressives, value the collectives in which their individual students belong; however, the pragmatic progressive sees himself as having an active relationship with those communities. Progressives, on the other hand, have an indirect relationship— assuming collectives will grow once students are fully whole, developed, and liberated.

It is through this active-inactive juxtaposition that standardized tests move from being an instrument of measurement to an instrument of communication for the pragmatic progressive. Through it, collectives can better understand the ways the hierarchy located *beyond* the schoolhouse is very well active and in play *within* the schoolhouse. It also shows how and what the dominant values as superior skills as portions of the test in which students of color outperform their White affluent counterparts are often minimized if not ignored (Willie, 2001). Finally, as to the first point, it shows a need to be superior, or (stated in a less provocative way) it shows how the dominant group stays the dominant group as the test is rewritten when historically disadvantaged students close the performance gaps within those tests. People misunderstand the test's relationship to the achievement gap. It is assumed that the test simply reveals a gap. Instead, by their sorting, separating, and ranking nature, we should accept that standardized tests are designed to actually create a gap.

In short, standardized tests report out the political states of students as related to race, class, and ability (physical and learning). They also communicate the competitive conditions in which students are instructed and the political priorities in which such instruction is grounded. Until the dominant group no longer governs the curriculum and instruction, we will continue to need assessments that unveil the group's deepest truths. Standardized tests provide this insight as they are about politics more so than they are about learning. The pragmatic progressive is committed to all conditions of learning, even those that are political. Simply put, standardized tests give insight into these conditions.

It should go without saying that political reporting isn't the only condition that should be generated and shared in education. Ultimately, collectives need to know what students are learning and how well they are learning it. But, for the pragmatic progressive, education is more than about learning. For marginalized collectives, it is also about power. Standardized tests are the most efficient way to guide the public's consciousness as to power —where it is most located and how it is distributed.

ACCOUNTABILITY

To account is to make a record of a particular area of responsibility. To be accountable is to give a report of that record based on an established expectation in order to justify choices (or decisions) made in relation to said responsibility. With these two definitions in mind, accountability is therefore a state of submitting to an established performance expectation by reporting on decisions and actions made. The final political shift that progressives need to make relates to this accountability. In order to better protect (and promote) the freedom, personhood, and creativity of the collectives in which individual students belong, there needs to be a commitment (if not conviction) to be accountable to the communities we purport to serve.

Many people think accountability is a bad word because of how it has been misrepresented as a vehicle for punishment. While accountability can have outcomes that may make some uncomfortable, if done correctly, it is never about punishment. When done correctly, accountability is about being personally and collectively vested in a particular outcome. For the pragmatic progressive, that outcome is about student progress as well as student achievement. Doing it correctly for the pragmatic progressive means accountability is multi-directional. Students are accountable to learning, and teachers (school officials in general) are accountable to teaching.

At its core, directionality is about power. In a pragmatic progressive space, power is shared so that accountability is shared. In my first book (Dye, 2012), I framed this dynamic as *shared accountability* (as in the seventh principle of my empowerment framework). In that text, I advocate for students' right and responsibility to hold themselves accountable, peers accountable, and yes, teachers accountable. It's not the purpose of this book to talk about the specifics of shared accountability as relating to my framework; however, it is being highlighted to introduce the notion that accountability is about the direction of power. And, for the pragmatic progressive that promotes shared accountability, it is about power that is multi-directional and not centralized (or even neutral).

It's hard to imagine a pure progressive who wants to centralize and control power because most progressives have an abhorrent reaction to the notion of power. They act as though if you deny power, then it doesn't exist. However, the opposite is in fact true. If you ignore the dynamics of power, you maintain its current distribution. In the traditional sense, power is top-down, it is scarce (creating win-loss competitions), and it is inherent in specific social roles (i.e. adulthood) and lacking in others (i.e. childhood). So when progressives act as though they don't have power to share, what they ultimately do is protect current structures of power, where they are, in fact, the protected benefactors of said power.

This denial of power, and therefore refusal to redistribute it, is what makes accountability a bad word for progressives. One day, a full-scale project is needed to take on this notion of power among progressives (in regards to their distaste of it). But for this current project, it only needs to be offered that power is redistributed in a pragmatic progressive space so that accountability can be shared. When it is shared, accountability is not about punishment as much as it is about ownership of (and submission to) an expectation in which end results are reported.

CONCLUSION AND CONSIDERATIONS

In one of the endless revisions to this book, it occurred to me that the pragmatic progressive is ultimately about bringing progressive education to collectives located at the margins. Unfortunately, I did not want to tackle it because it was an idea that had critical, political implications. I would be forced to explore the capacity for progressives to really serve communities who have been historically underserved. And in doing so, I would have to poke at the political privileges of progressives and talk honestly about why they ironically are not able to present a progressive agenda to communities who need it the most.

When I was going through the writing process of my first book, I sent individual chapters to different people and invited their critique. In the chapter on project-based learning, one reviewer argued that I needed to address a community of educators who believed African-American students were not successful with that method. In that I had just successfully ran a project-based learning school for low-income African-American students for five years, I was initially offended by such a proposition. Over time (and research), I understood more of what he was trying to say. There are very few true project-based learning programs where Black and low-income students thrive. This failure, however, has nothing to do with the inherent state of learners. The failure is in the disconnect of those who are trying to serve them and their unwillingness to leave their own place of privilege.

A discussion on race and class is really required to make a case on the barriers that prevent progressives from successfully serving students at the margins. Until that conversation is had, the political shifts listed in this chapter (and the tactical shifts listed in the next) will help regardless of the political disconnection that might exist between progressive educators and their learners.

In closing, the pragmatic progressive is a progressive. He is flexible and he is interdependent with the collectives he teaches. Finally, he understands how to modify instruction so as to meet students where they are and value what they offer the learning process from that position.

3

TACTICAL SHIFTS OF THE
PRAGMATIC PROGRESSIVE

I n the previous chapter, I twice referenced my first book. *Empowerment Starts Here: Seven Principles to Empowering Urban Youth* (2012) was written, from an organizational lens, to showcase my approach (and commitment) to promoting the individual and collective freedom, personhood, and creativity of my students. Without being identified, it is truly where the pragmatic progressive made its debut. Framed around seven principles for student empowerment (later clarified in my dissertation as multiple literacies), the book shows how I achieved these desired outcomes along with other progressive ideals (student independence, authentic learning, and strong classroom relationships) across the school. The unstated value of the book, however, is that not only did I show the school-level implementation of progressive themes, but I also showed the side-by-side implementation of more practical mandates. These mandates, more aligned with traditional practice, ultimately painted a picture of the powerful marriage between progressivism and traditionalism; and together, pragmatic progressivism (as a philosophy and as a methodology) was born!

The beauty of the union between progressivism and traditionalism (also respected as behaviorism) cannot be overstated. In terms of popular approaches to educational practice, progressivism and behaviorism are known to be ideologically at odds. Progressivism often supports constructivism which centers the learner and protects the power of the learner to make meaning of his learning, to create knowledge, and to be co-conductors of the teaching and learning process alongside of his teachers. On the other hand, behaviorism often supports instructivism which protects the notion that knowledge is independent and context free, that learning requires a set of prescribed behaviors amongst learners (and teachers for that matter), and that student behaviors are indicative of student learning (which, at times, is a reasonable premise, but not always scientifically true). So, while it has been argued that these two schools of thought are counterintuitive and hard to be accepted as ideologically compatible, *Empowerment Starts Here* (2012) showed that such a marriage is possible.

The book I am presenting now, on the other hand, was written to do something different. Instead of showing the marriage of two competing philosophies, I decided to give specific attention to the practical treatments needed when those two philosophies are blended as one singular practice. Such attention thereby requires us to look more intently, and willingly, at behaviorism (traditional ideals and methods many progressives have denounced). Particularly as relating to this chapter, I want to offer some tactical changes pragmatic progressives make to strengthen our progressive commitment to individual students and the collectives in which they live.

BEHAVIORISM AS PROTECTION

Much of what is currently understood as practical tactics of the pragmatic progressive has been lifted out of the practices of three teachers from my dissertation. Identified in a two-tiered process as being highly effective (for empowering low-income, African-American students), these teachers beautifully highlighted four strategies that are essential for the work. It is for this reason that I am using their practice to showcase traditional strategies necessary for the pragmatic side of pragmatic progressivism.

As stated in the previous chapter, I created a student-power construct because my dissertation revealed a gap in the treatment of students as agents of power. I mostly focus on the student-power gap as a condition embedded within my empowerment framework, as unveiled in my first book (Dye, 2012). However, there was another (related) condition of student powerlessness the dissertation revealed and it was in the practice of those three teachers who had been identified as successful. The state of their success within a condition of powerlessness actually makes a case against behaviorism all while the pragmatic side of pragmatic progressivism depends on it. In order to properly position behaviorism within the pragmatic side of the practice, I first need to delimit its value. To this end, I want to talk briefly about the powerlessness of behaviorism alone.

In short, my research was about identifying ways successful teachers empower disadvantaged students. To collect data, I used my student empowerment framework, which provided seven distinct ways in which teachers help students build power, share power, and resist power. As I entered into the data collection process, I immediately noticed two things. First, it was obvious why these teachers had been first recommended (by people in their community) and then validated (by their school principals) as being successful. They consistently used strategies that were connected to three of the power-building principles of the framework (Principle 1 [achievement is based on mindset], Principle 3 [achievement is based on skill], and Principle 5 [achievement is based on responsibility]). The second thing I noticed (as already stated) was that there was an absence of true student power. In spite of seeing nuances of student empowerment, I ultimately could not see actual student power. This realization that an existence of best practice can, at the same time, be prohibitive of student power created cognitive dissonance at best.

In my attempt to resolve the conflict, the notion of student power as a separate and unique feature within student empowerment was created. In future texts, I will unveil the intricacies of the student-power construct; however, for now, know there are four distinct components of that construct which make clear that students at all times, exclusively through their agency, should learn as an act of transforming their world. In order to protect this agency, an infrastructure is needed to guard its role in the learning process. This agency protecting infrastructure is where behaviorism has value, and as is the critical point of this chapter, four specific strategies essential to this process will be presented.

STANDARDS, LEARNING OBJECTIVES, AND DAILY TARGETS

While the teachers in my dissertation research did not center students' power in the learning process, they did provide students with the *what* and even the *why* for learning. This what-and-why is essential for student power and offers a clear distinction between the progressive and the pragmatic progressive. Pragmatic progressives borrow from the progressives in unfixing the science of teaching. Through the science of teaching, instruction is governed by grade-level standards as a methodical approach to reach an end state (condition) of learning.

Pragmatic progressives, just like progressives, lean into the art of teaching by partnering with students (driven by their readiness and interest levels) to co-create learning targets. Learning targets, or any concrete focus on the what-and-why to learning, give students access to two important ends. First, it allows them to clearly articulate what they learned (as opposed to what they performed), strengthening pathways for storage, retrieval of knowledge, and (more importantly) the transfer and application of that knowledge into different and broader contexts. Second, the what-and-why to learning gives students power as, in the storage-retrieval-transfer-application process, students are able to access their learning utility (as in tools of power) and willfully, with agency, use it to achieve and solve problems as needed.

Students cannot co-create these learning targets if teachers have not first defined the aims for learning (the standards). As a result, standards are essential to pragmatic progressives. But often, as is the reason they are not always supported by progressives, school leaders dictate a focus on daily learning objectives as the only means to achieve those standards. These daily objectives are driven by the agency of the teacher (even justice-oriented teachers) and leave out the agency of the learner. Between teacher agency and administrative mandates, teaching becomes fixed and the art of teaching, to meet the human needs and interest of the student, is never realized.

When I started writing this book, I was firmly in the practice of having clearly established learning objectives to center the learning environment and guide instruction. For ten years before I moved into school leadership and for the ten years after, I was a huge proponent of the power that comes from telling students what they are going to learn and reminding them along the way what they are learning while they are learning it. I do not say what I did in the past to suggest that I no longer believe in using learning objectives to center and guide learning. I will say that now, having a more justice orientation than I had before, I have found myself leaning more into my progressive orientation—centering students first and then using learning objectives second to frame the learning process.

In Chapter 5, I will talk with you about my return to the classroom. After doing leadership and being in the field for 15 years, I took a 6th grade assignment. Ironically, through this self-imposed assignment (read the fifth chapter to learn more about the imposition of it all), I noticed a shift in my orientation towards learning objectives. Before my fieldwork, I was a huge proponent of daily objectives. As already stated, I believed they were essential to getting students to a desired state of knowing. I had to learn to highlight skills and concepts as part of my daily objectives, but, with or without that focus, those daily objectives have always defined my practice. However, after having the jurisdiction to design learning to meet the needs of students, I moved away from daily objectives and, instead, provided students with weekly objectives. Through this shift from daily to weekly (or biweekly depending on the level of learning), I invited students into the learning design process. It is here that students started creating their own daily objectives (what I am now calling targets). When I returned to the classroom after that experience, I simply could not go back to controlling the daily process for learning. I needed to let students control it based on their grade-level readiness and interests. Yes, we were still on target for the grade-level standards and, as with the teacher informants that contributed to my dissertation, we had a clear daily focus on isolated concepts and skills. The difference was that students were empowered to be co-agents of power and, with me as their partner, they created their focus for the day.

SKILL ARTICULATION AND REINFORCEMENT

Along the lines of having clearly established learning objectives (governed by standards and reinforced by student-driven learning targets) is a commitment to articulate and reinforce those objectives. This is what the teachers in my dissertation demonstrated beautifully. As I observed them, I knew instinctively they were empowering students with the knowledge of instruction—and not simply with the knowledge of content. This knowing about instruction *and* content (also understood as curriculum) is what is called cognitivism.

Cognitivism is a learning theory that says students better learn when they know more about what they are learning and why. While behaviorism focuses on the stimuli and behaviors of learning and progressivism focuses on the human conditions of (and for) learning, cognitivism bridges the two. It makes way for students' need to know what they are learning, how they will be learning it, and the whys to it all. Pragmatic progressivism is deeply ensconced in cognitivism because it empowers students with the what, the how, and the why. Only by stating (and restating) the learning objectives does the work of cognitivism begin. The teachers in my study were clearly committed to this part of instruction. They named and articulated the objectives, posted the objectives, and reminded students of those objectives along the way.

Not only did the teachers in the study reinforce learning objectives by engaging in a continuous articulation-loop, they also articulated the behavioral expectations associated with such learning and then established an economy of consequences. Now, the moment I say the word consequence, the reader should immediately think behaviorism as it suggests that external stimuli are being added to enforce a particular behavior. And this is true. Negatively or positively, external stimuli are being applied for the sole purpose of impacting behavior. The teachers in my dissertation research had this reinforcement mastered. Whether it was a behavior chart hanging on a wall aligned with a very active behavior management system, physical trinkets distributed during class, or verbal praise and redirection, the teachers were committed to reinforcing the behavioral expectations of their students.

In that the pragmatic progressive is more of a constructivist than a behaviorist, I am not suggesting that we bypass tenets we hold true about deep learning or those borrowed from reconstructivism that champion student dignity (to be discussed in the next chapter). Deep learning and student dignity remain at the forefront of pragmatic progressivism; however, alongside these values is an understanding that students need the opportunity to actually learn more about the behaviors that are associated with deep learning and dignity. That is what the teachers from my dissertation modeled. They were building student awareness and consciousness of what it means to achieve. The pragmatic progressive, also committed to the achievement of students (albeit defined and framed around power), must likewise help students build an awareness and consciousness around the behaviors that promote dignity and deep learning as well as those behaviors that detract from them. This awareness is a central piece to a student-power infrastructure.

FLOOR SPACE AND STUDENT PROXIMITY

Another behavioral way to protect student power is to use floor space. The teachers in my dissertation were continuously walking among students so as to check their work and redirect them immediately (as opposed to waiting for the work to be turned in for an assessment). They also walked amongst the students as a preventative method, in that some students were less likely to get off task with the teacher standing close by as a reminder of what is expected. If a student was having a side conversation with his tablemate, the teacher would just go and stand next to the table and more than likely, the student would stop. No words were necessary from the teacher. His body—his presence—alone served as a redirection.

In many ways, the progressive educator would see this floor usage as oppressive. Similar to how overseers use to keep field hands in line, a progressive educator would not want to use his body to intimidate learners to stay focused on their work. It is for this reason that I need to be clear. The pragmatic progressive also holds this view and works hard to not serve as a looming force of intimidation; yet, the pragmatic progressive tells students that they do not need to be intimidated nor bullied in order to learn. Here is where cognitivism comes into play again. A progressive educator may simply give students the space to choose—a worthy strategy in that making good choices is a skill that needs practice and freedom. But a pragmatic progressive will teach students about making good choices as a practice and about the freedom needed to make poor choices. And with the consequences discussed in the previous section, a conversation is needed that makes students aware of the ways they are practicing and using this freedom.

In that I have talked about the negative usage of floor space and student proximity, the reader may wonder why it has even been mentioned as a strategy for student power. A critical strategy of liberatory practice is dialogue. Allowing students to talk side-by-side with teachers changes the power structure from power-over to power with. Only through a shared power dialogue can teachers learn more about the human self (and needs) of the student. Students and teachers, in proximity to one another, are able to dialogue and share ideas—to learn from one another— and together, strengthen the pathways for higher-order processing. I mention floor space because it is here that students are in proximity with their teacher for a dialogical relationship. Instead of using the floor to intimidate and bully students to do their work, or, in a not so charged way, to redirect students back to doing their work, the pragmatic progressive is close by engaging with students on a human level.

VISION AND COMMITMENT BUILDING

The last tactical shift to discuss as relating to the pragmatic progressive is vision work and it is like effective writing. *Tell them what you are going to say; say what you are going to say; and then remind them of what you have already said.* I have heard this advice time and time again as a writer and I think it is ultimately about centering writing within the connection the author has with the reader. The person reading the text wants to know what's in it for me (WIFM) and often, if not always, he makes the choice to read because he knows (clearly or intuitively) it would be a good use of his time.

When we truly appreciate students as agents of power, and not just agents of compliance and consumption, we will apply the advice given to writers. Whether it is a reader or a learner, agents of power need to be respected for the resources they do and do not bring to the table. Time is a resource; focus is a resource; and energy is a resource. The learner, as well as the reader, should not be taken for granted as if their time, focus, and energy are automatic guarantees in our relationships with them. As pragmatic progressives, we must ask, if not compete, for their time, focus and energy. There is no better way to do this than to clearly articulate what you are offering and why.

Vision work for the pragmatic progressive is about motivation and must include the *what* and the *why*. It is more than a learning objective (although it absolutely must include one) and it is more than context and relevance (which also must be included). It is about activating students into their tomorrow... right now. Students spend so much time as children being cut off from their own agency that when it is time to think about their future, they inadvertently feel as though they are thinking about someone else's future. It is not really that students cannot see themselves in the future. They cannot see themselves as independent actors. Without vision work, the future they see belongs to someone else; and, as a result, their motivation to care about learning is minimal (if at all). They simply cannot find the motivation to care about a future in which they are not intrinsically connected.

A pragmatic progressive motivates the learner through vision work by connecting students to their tomorrow. Therefore, instruction—by way of their personhood, their cognitive wiring, and their internal resources (time, focus, energy)—must include this vision work. Within this vision work, students need to be told clearly what they are going to learn and why they should learn it. It should be clear so they can choose it. The condition of being clear cannot be oversold as it is here that students can act as agents of power and choose, select, and apply what is learned as they desire. When the what-and-why to learning is ambiguous, congested, or complicated, students may not choose to learn—all while choosing something else as a different set of options have now become available (with or without our intention).

It needs to be stated that an integral part of vision building is commitment building. For the pragmatic progressive, this commitment is not really about the student. It is about the teacher! Not only do students need to be connected to learning by a future that connects to them at their core, but they also need to see instruction that connects with their teachers at *their* core. This connection is about your convictions. It is about why you teach; why you teach those particular students; and why you are teaching *that* particular lesson. It is here in the conviction that houses the magic for motivation and buy-in. It is where the line between teacher and student erases. It is where students know that they are human because they can see their humanness in you. You become the reflection of what the world has tried to hide —their goodness; their value; their purpose; their agency.

While I think their vision and their commitment were not fully aligned with my political views on student and community empowerment, the teachers in my study modeled this part of the pragmatic progressive perfectly. Their instruction was loaded with the whats and whys to learning and their students were motivated and bought into their lessons as a result. This is the shift that you need to make to become a pragmatic progressive. You must dig down to the core of your human self and connect it to the core human self of your students. You must select and present learning objectives relevant for a tomorrow that they are experiencing right now! And, you must respect them as agents of power, knowing what they will be and are already. These truths, all of them without exceptions, will make your instruction WIFM ready.

CONCLUSION AND CONSIDERATIONS

It cannot be overstated that the only way the treatment of student power could have been framed is by way of the three teacher-informants of my dissertation. Through their consistent use of best-practices, the presence of student-powerlessness was amplified. And, it is here that we understand that best-practice alone does not necessarily automate students as subjects (agents) of power; as a result, best practices (mostly championed by traditionalists) should only be embraced inside of a progressive agenda (a pragmatic progressive agenda to be more exact).

One of my greatest regrets with my dissertation was that I was not able to highlight the four strengths of the teacher informants of my study and the powerful impact they had on me understanding my very own framework. Being consumed with the absence of student power, and actually conceptualizing its absence, what worked well in their teaching took the backseat to what was missing. I hope this chapter did what my 300(plus) page dissertation could not. I hope it showed their value. Through them, we were truly provided with models for the pragmatic side of pragmatic progressivism!

4

PHILOSOPHICAL BOOKENDS

In the previous chapter, I talk about tactical shifts necessary for pragmatic progressivism. Much of that discussion was grounded in behaviorism as purposed for the pragmatic side of the practice. In this chapter, however, I want to talk more about the philosophy of pragmatic progressivism as a unified concept (which includes talking more about behaviorism). Doing so better positions the pragmatic progressive for the real work of application in which he must contend.

There are two philosophical extremes that the pragmatic progressive must confront: behaviorism and social reconstructionism. Of course the pragmatic progressive must also confront progressivism but for the sake of this discussion, progressivism has been aligned with constructivism and will be contrasted against the two ends in which pragmatic progressivism is encased. In the end, it is important to consider how the pragmatic progressive navigates between the two philosophies as such navigation will make him (as in social reconstructionism) or break him (as in behaviorism). In the next segment, I will begin the conversation by diving more deeply into behaviorism as it is the most familiar, and the most threatening, of the two.

BEHAVIORISM

Behaviorism is a school of thought that simply reasons learning to be the direct response (change) to specific (and particularly arranged) stimuli. In most schools, you see this philosophy manifest in four ways. The first manifestation of behaviorism at the school level relates to the construct of knowledge. In behaviorism, knowledge is predetermined and it is universal. In constructivism, however, knowledge is created and it is local. The difference between the two treatments of knowing depends on different beliefs concerning power. Constructivism is when you believe that power is inherently in all of us. As a constructivist, you will believe that everyone has the power to know; everyone has the power to make meaning (make new knowledge); and everyone has the power to share that knowledge with others. Behaviorism, however, is different. Behaviorism is when you believe power is a dividend of an elite class or resides in a universal or outside entity (such as God or nature). With this outsourcing of power, you believe knowledge is predetermined (as opposed to created); outside-in (as opposed to inside-out); and passed along under special circumstances (as opposed to passed along because in general, it is a continuous, evolving entity).

The second manifestation of behaviorism at the school level relates to the position and purpose of teachers. If knowledge is predetermined and accessed only in a prescribed manner, then teachers are certified authorities of such prescription. Teachers go to school to become experts on knowing and experts on the way such knowing should be transferred. While many would argue that behaviorism centers the teacher, a more accurate depiction is to say that behaviorism actually centers knowledge. With this treatment, teachers are simply authorized agents for funneling such knowledge and depositing it into the minds of the students. It is important to note that even though teachers are not technically centered in a behaviorist environment, it appears to be so all the same. This perception is then reinforced due to their training and the public narratives we hold and circulate about them. In that teachers are certified power holders of knowledge, their position, by default, becomes centered.

The third manifestation of behaviorism at the school level relates to the role of students. If behaviorism centers knowledge (as linked to an ultimate outside authority) and teachers are arbiters of that knowledge (as powered through a certification process), then students, in terms of the teaching and learning process, have very little power. Therefore, regardless of what they learn and regardless of what they do in order to learn, behaviorism maintains their powerlessness. This distinction on position and power for students is important in light of reform movements that try to implement tenets from constructivism without disrupting the ultimate philosophy (and structure) of behaviorism. Despite classroom activities, behaviorism essentially moves power in one direction (top down) and positions students at the end of that direction (the bottom), making them receivers of knowing and not agents of knowing.

There are *progressive* spaces, perceived to be more culturally relevant, that are still driven by principles of behaviorism. In this practice, teachers create instruction that connects with students' context and supposes to give them voice and choice along the way. In many ways, these environments are moving students closer to the position and power of teachers, but it should be clearly stated that, first, they do not ever align to share the same plane of power. Second, neither of them, teachers nor students, are really in positions of power as relating to knowing and learning as both are controlled by an outside entity that dictates what knowing and learning is. Third, and is really the most essential, the context of the learner is defined by a power distribution of the outside world. Bringing in that world as context does nothing to disrupt power and for students in the margins, there is an inherited state of powerlessness that is reinforced and solidified by a power hoarding learning model. Teachers are simply allowing students to recognize, present, and choose knowledge that has already been created for them. Very little of the knowledge that students create (through the state of their own subjectivity) is assessed and showcased in this reward-driven system of behaviorism (although it masks itself as culturally relevant instruction).

And this leads to the fourth and last manifestation of behaviorism at the school level that needs to be highlighted before moving on: consequences—rewards and punishments. As already stated, behaviorism is a belief system that says learning is a result of ordered stimuli. Learning in this system must be observable, which means there must be a visible change in the behavior of students. To encourage, reinforce, or require such change, additional stimuli are then provided in the form of rewards and punishments. Students learn early on what knowing is rewarded and what knowing is punished. A constructivist environment functions differently. It respects students as agents of knowing. It creates instruction that invites students to build identities as knowing agents (a type of knowing that actually disrupts oppressive identities). It also gives students more choices in how they are able to know. Constructivism, not behaviorism, disrupts the power structure and positionality of students so that students are more than responders to stimuli. They are creators of stimuli.

The Conflict and Cost of Embracing a Few Tenets of Behaviorism

For the pragmatic progressive, as first discussed in the previous chapter, behaviorism has a valued role. However, instead of rewards and punishment being used to reinforce the traditional power structure, they are used to reinforce a new power structure. Students are therefore celebrated when they are constructors of knowledge and redirected when they, alone, are not. The pragmatic progressive will have to fight to walk this fine line between behaviorism that empowers and behaviorism that oppresses. To do so would be to borrow only a few tenets of behaviorism as opposed to borrowing only a few tenets of constructivism. The only part of behaviorism that has value for the pragmatic progressive, but is important all the same, is the part that reinforces a new paradigm for knowing. Such reinforcement rewards and redirects so that students can identify and act as agents of knowing.

It is important to share that behaviorist environments can borrow tenets of constructivism so much that actors in that environment can believe the environment to be constructivist or even in route to constructivism. However, in order for an environment to be really constructivist in nature, it must move beyond tenets of constructivism where knowledge, teachers, and students are perceived in a particular way. It must have an actual structure for constructivism that generates, protects, and sustains itself. As a scholar of power, I am aware that very little attention is given to power structures in general. Power structures are the invisible forces that are responsible for the visible; however, most people are distracted, occupied, or even lulled by the visible. In a behaviorist environment, there are power structures that maintain traditionalism and make constructivism an act (on a good day) or a stress point (on a common day). Such power structures are captured by policies (such as the number of Carnegie hours of instruction), facilities and operations (where and how students and teachers interact), and revenue and budgets (how monies are collected, disbursed and used to support instruction)—all of which are expensive.

As an experienced school executive, I know constructivism to be costly not because the application of constructivism practices is more expensive but the conjoint application of constructivism alongside required traditional practice is expensive. In a constructivist environment, teachers and students must have different constructions of *teacher* and *student*, different construction of *facilities* and *operations*, and different constructions of *policies*. Frankly, it is less expensive to do one or the other —either a behaviorist model or a constructivist model. It is more expensive to employ them both. And, while tenets of constructivism may be permitted in a behaviorist environment—or even desired—a behaviorist environment will never lose its grips on traditional structures —thereby creating an expensive, and, often, an ideologically conflicted learning space.

The Part that Matters

Before moving to the next section, let me add that constructivism disrupts traditional power and positionality of students so that students are more than emerging arbiters of knowledge (as are their teachers) but are constructors of knowledge. Likewise, before a teacher can do this disruption for his students, he must be able to do it for himself. An oppressed person without such deconstruction cannot liberate another. Only a psychologically liberated person can. This ultimate point on liberation is why only a fraction of behaviorism can be utilized by the pragmatic progressive. It is strictly the part that carves out, identifies, rewards and reinforces freedom.

SOCIAL RECONSTRUCTIONISM

The talk about disrupting teachers' power and positionality in the classroom, particularly in requiring them to be agents of knowing and not just arbiters of knowing, lends itself perfectly to this next section on social reconstructionism. Earlier in this chapter, I said there were two poles of thinking in which the pragmatic progressive must contend—that will either make or break him as a pragmatic progressive. Being more aligned with constructivism, the pragmatic progressive must first confront the nature of behaviorism as this pole of the spectrum presents the greatest risks. If a teacher cannot know *with* the student but most know *for* the student, constructivism will not survive. If a student cannot make meaning but can only receive and store meaning, constructivism will not survive. If knowledge is a predetermined entity of an elite class, thereby giving credence to the misrepresented proverb, *knowledge is power* (as opposed to knowledge making is power), then constructivism will not survive.

But, a pragmatic progressive does not stop at constructivism. Being a pragmatic progressive is more than allowing teachers and students to travel together as knowers and meaning-makers. It is more than localizing knowledge and giving visibility to the utility for which it was constructed. A pragmatic progressive has an agenda as pertaining to the outside world—like all methods or philosophies of education. For the pragmatic progressive, teaching and learning are not only a set of methods but a philosophical orientation that allows teachers to move in a particular direction even when—or particularly when—there is not a prescription for it. This philosophical orientation is situated in social reconstructionism where there is an acute awareness of the sociopolitical world beyond prescriptive knowing, teaching, and learning. With this understanding, knowledge is not just something generated at the personal level (adult or child; certified or not); it is something that is created to serve a sociopolitical agenda. We often do not think about agendas when they serve us but only when they begin to serve someone else —especially the someone else that has been historically overlooked. This is why social reconstructionists are seen to be radicals because they promote an agenda that is focused on the historically erased or disenfranchised.

The standard definition for social reconstructionism is that it is an education philosophy that positions schools to solve a social problem. While the pragmatic progressive concedes to this definition, it recognizes that all schooling has been designed to solve a social problem since the beginning of time.

The Social Agenda in Context

Before the start of institutionalized education, wealthy individuals educated their children in private, primarily by way of tutors. However, as a need emerged for national loyalty and a trained workforce for the nation's economy, institutionalized schooling emerged. This evolution is the first example of how schooling has been positioned to serve a social agenda. Another example is exploring the education of African-American children.

During the colonial period, African Americans sought segregated schools because their children were not safe or getting adequate education while being educated with White children. In the mid 19th-century, Booker T. Washington argued for an educated, African-American workforce (as opposed to the argument of W. E. B. Dubois that African Americans needed leadership and intellectual freedom more than they needed jobs). And then at the early part of the 20th century, African-American southerners privately financed the education of their youth (all while being taxed for the education of White children). Even in more recent years, with the now reformed No Child Left Behind policy, schooling continues to serve a social agenda and that is in the form of college and career readiness (as driven by tests).

What makes pragmatic progressivism different from social reconstructionism is that it reasons that schooling has always had a social agenda. To argue for a social problem solving utility of schools obscures the social problem creation of schools. In short, schools have created social problems more than they have solved them, thereby, exacerbating other social problems. To delimit social reconstructionism to social problem solving seems almost deceptive. Another challenge of social reconstructionism is the means by its centric positioning of democratic principles. While pragmatic progressivism favors those principles more than unfavors them, it does recognize the way democratic traditions maintain the status quo more than disrupts the status quo. As a wrap-up, the pragmatic progressive practice challenges social reconstructionism in two ways. First, it does not position schooling as a social problem solving instrument without acknowledging the schooling as a social problem creation instrument. Second, it takes a clear stance that oppression is the social problem in which it wants to solve and is committed to disrupting systems of oppression even when such oppression is the result of democratic principles.

EQUITY AS THE ULTIMATE AGENDA

There is a tenet from social reconstructionism that has significant value and therefore has been placed as the back bookend to pragmatic progressivism. It reminds the pragmatic progressive that education is about hidden social agendas and, therefore, forces the educator to decide which agenda he wants to promote. Other educators can become conveniently unconcerned about the social agenda of schooling because it does not cause discomfort to be an agent for such an agenda or because the agenda itself benefits them. The pragmatic progressive, on the other hand, looks for the social agenda even when, or especially when, it is invisible and critically examines who the agenda advantages and disadvantages.

With this praxis in mind, the awareness of and the search for agenda inequities, the pragmatic progressive chooses instructional methods (not just ideologies) that disrupt those inequities and instills a more equitable practice. And here is where the *by any means necessary* disposition of Lisa Delpit, Gloria Ladson-Billings, and the Late Marva Collins ring true. The pragmatic progressive does not have fidelity to an instructional model… not even to pragmatic progressivism. He has fidelity to social equity. With this instructional agenda, any method—measurable/unmeasurable, scientific/unscientific—has value.

CONCLUSION AND CONSIDERATIONS

Overall, the pragmatic progressive requires us to take a look at three philosophies of education: behaviorism first, constructivism second, social reconstructionism third. But it is important to end this chapter with how the pragmatic progressive transcends all three schools of thought because 1) it confronts the individual and society in a way that is different than all three and 2) it is concerned with the application of philosophy as it is committed to promoting change (measurably, not just theoretically, speaking). As a result, the pragmatic progressive not only aims to solve a social problem but intrinsically feels a moral conviction to do so. In this conviction, and as a reminder, the following concepts are constructs that need their own distinction:

- **Knowing**: Knowing is about utility. In short, it *is* because it *does*. If knowing performs a critical function, it is safe to accept it as knowledge. In saying this, and in juxtaposing knowledge from the pragmatic progressive's point of view against the traditionalist's or social reconstructionist's point of view, knowledge is both local and universal. Admittedly, it is ultimately local, derived from a specific context for a specific purpose; however, once it is formed, it can live beyond its immediate context and beyond its specific purpose to serve an aim not previously imagined. To this end, it does not matter how knowledge was formed. What matters is that it can serve a purpose.

- **Teaching**: Teaching is about transformation. While the pragmatic progressive sees teaching as impacting the perspective, judgment, and behaviors of the learner, it does not limit teaching to either the behaviorist's point of view (where the teacher transfers preconceived knowing) or the constructivist's point of view (where the teacher creates an environment so the learner can be the knower and the meaning maker). The pragmatic progressive sees the teacher as the tour guide that will get the learner to his destination. In that the pragmatic progressive has, like the social reconstructionist, a social agenda, his ultimate aim is to expand the learner's toolbox with the ability to both create knowing and use someone else's knowing effectively.

- **Student**: Students, for the pragmatic progressive, are budding agents of change. They are not only learners for the sake of consuming or building new knowledge but they are also future change agents, furthering the evolution of the human condition. Under the guidance of a teacher, they are simply expanding their toolbox of knowing and their strategies for doing (as related to change agentry).

5

WHAT'S NEXT

In Chapter One, I talked about a phone conversation I had with Marva Collins who influenced my thinking on the pragmatic progressive. As stated, I was the founding executive director of a charter school and I was trying to confront the politics of the job. In that call, Ms. Collins challenged me not to succumb to the politics; not to take on someone else's agenda as my own; not to forget my beliefs about the children I am serving or my commitment to them; and finally, not to limit my work to pre-existing paradigms of service. Her charge was that taking on the mission for serving children does not have to be in the role of a teacher, a school leader, or anything we have traditionally understood.

This is the point in which I want to end the book. The pragmatic progressive is not about a philosophy or even a method as much as it is about a mission. The pragmatic progressive wants to see children, and the communities that house them, in a space where they are able "to produce, to prosper, and to promote growth in themselves and in others" (language taken directly from my first book, *Empowerment Starts Here [Dye, 2012]* , p. 7). In this achievement orientation for children and their communities, the pragmatic progressive is a by-any-means-necessary practitioner and will only use the tenets of this book as a guide—not as a limitation. Even better, the pragmatic progressive is focused on this achievement aim (production, prosperity and the promotion of growth) and does not stop until it becomes an outcome.

TAKE TWO

As a classroom teacher back in the day, I did not have access to quantitative data to demonstrate contemporary achievement outcomes. Influenced by the schooling of that time period, I was of the mindset that classroom climate, student engagement, student relationships, and instructional creativity were qualitative indicators of effectiveness. It is true that as an emerging pragmatic progressive back then, I wanted to excel by way of these indicators; however, I wanted more of what represented change... even if I did not know how to measure the change I was seeking. As I matured in both my philosophy of education and my convictions in change agentry, I found myself entertaining an opportunity to design, start, and manage my own charter school. Spiritually, I had resolved that the curriculum I had been developing along the way made room for learning and change; therefore, moving the curriculum into a school model seemed the right thing to do.

Starting the school was my *take two*. I was able to take all that I had learned about pragmatic progressivism from being a teacher and move it beyond the classroom. I was able to see what else was possible when I not only had influence on the culture, curriculum, and classroom procedures but also on the culture, curriculum, and procedures of staff and community stakeholders as well. So, with knowing much about students, curriculum and instruction yet knowing very little about starting a business, I opened and operated my very first school. For five years, I earnestly pursued the vision of the pragmatic progressive and by the time of the closing, here is what I quantitatively reported to the public ...

- We took a group of students with a track record of making .36 annual gains (when spending seven years in the traditional school) to making 1.33 annual gains (after spending five years at my school).
- We outperformed the district in all core subject areas in 2009 and outperformed schools with similar demographics (racial and poverty levels) in the other years.

- We maintained a safe learning environment where less than .004% of students were suspended for violent weapons compared to the district's 1-3%.
- We generated a school climate where 100% of students felt safe, as reported on the district's annual survey.
- We engaged 100% of students (including those who were at least 3.5 grade levels behind) in a higher-order thinking process where students, via project based learning, explored global problems and developed local solutions.

Because I did not have the sophistication (or the confidence), I did not report on our qualitative achievements. Had I had the wherewithal, I would have added the following to my reporting...

- In the first year (as measured) and in subsequent years (as not measured), our students had a Hope indicator score that exceeded all other schools who used that system of measurement. [Note: The indicator score correlated with student persistence and efficacy throughout life.]
- Our students had a deep understanding of the social world and a keen sense on how they could strategically work to solve some of its key social problems.

- Our students came to our school feeling broken and disconnected from this thing that we call schooling but left feeling whole with identities of being leaders and scholars.
- Our students needed resources to further the experience we had given them to be scholars, leaders, change agents; and, they needed an agency, not a school, who could partner with them as they continued on in their journey.

In all, I am proud of that which was reported to the public; however, I am more proud and committed to that which was not. As already implicated, I only kept the school open for the length of its contract. After five years, I knew there was more that I wanted to do and I had to honestly ask myself if the current partnership, or better state the current contract, lent itself to the true vision. When I realized the answer was no, I entered into joint negotiations with our authorizer to close. It is important to note that the authorizer at the time was actually closing seven of its schools but I was the only one who did not campaign to stay open. Whereas I had a compelling case to stay open (with measurable and competitive data), I did not want to give five more years to a truncated version of the vision. In other words, staying open in its current iteration would have been winning to lose. The partnership simply did not offer the right infrastructure (politically, financially, and contractually speaking) to truly position the school as an agency of change.

After I closed the school, I got really busy trying to understand how my role as an educator could honestly be a part of social change. I returned to my curriculum and upgraded it with all that I learned from my *take two*. I better understood the social emotional needs of my target population and strengthened the curriculum's ability to one day serve students who have not just been left behind but to serve those who have been victimized by social-structural oppression (**and** a toxic school reform agenda that also harms them). I then went on to write a book about the curriculum, the school, and my experience as its founder. And lastly, I returned to school and earned a PhD to learn more about the instructional needs of my target population (particularly around power, race, class, and learning).

With the curriculum, the book, and the PhD behind me, I finally understood my work in social change agentry. I had completed a short stint as an executive director of another charter school and had a chance to see the positive impact of my pragmatic progressive model beyond the school that I started. This impact provided confirmation that my curriculum is still very much a central part of my work as a change agent.

THE UNRETURN

I am currently prepping for my *take three*. While I am not yet at liberty to completely divulge the plan, I can say there is a plan and it is in the continuation of my commitment to pragmatic progressivism. Interestingly enough, this book, and me finally getting it done, is a public admission that there will be, in fact, a *take three*. When this chapter was first written, I had finally taken a day job as a sixth-grade teacher in a large urban school district. I initially perceived this position to be a perfect place to serve until my *take three* was ready. I was looking for work that would give me pleasure, all while allowing me to take a break from executive-level leadership. While this position gave me immense joy, it actually did not allow me to take a break from executive-level leadership. Quite surprisingly, it showed me that executive-level leadership is, and forever will be, an essential part of my work.

First, I realized that I am a movement-based practitioner. After completing my doctorate, I spent three years as an adjunct in higher education at two predominately White institutions (PWIs)—teaching teachers at the graduate level and sociologist at the undergraduate level. While these positions gave me delicious (and truly, there is no better descriptor) access to theory, I came to realize that they did not give me access to movement—structural movement that is. As a social change agent, my strength (and passion) is in disrupting systems that maintain the status quo. Interestingly, those two places where I served as an adjunct were not committed to disruption. In fact, I distinctly heard some co-workers say they do not want to disrupt. With the social unrest that has erupted over the past decade, I am deeply confused (if not concerned) by those who do not see disruption as part of the change process (although I do understand that refraining from disruption sometimes is a necessary response to fatigue).

It is with this confusion (and concern) that one of my friends also in higher education gave me my second realization—that my movement work is specifically with minority-based student communities (especially around race and class). Out of all of my friends who are in higher education, she is the only one who defined the work by standards of race. Having also been employed at a PWI, she eventually left to go teach at a historically Black college or university (HBCU). Since then, she and I have talked about others who have not left. While they are also challenged by maintenance work, they resolve the conflict by staying at their PWIs and privately bemoaning the microaggressions they experience. As my friend and I both agreed, this approach is not the solution. There is no change in complaining.

This friend, the one who departed from her PWI precisely because it was a PWI, challenges me to think more about race and class in the movement work I want to do. With this realization (that race and class are part of my work as a change agent), the local urban district, which has a minority-majority (and a substantial low-income) student population, caught my attention. While I knew I could not do the type of movement work I did when I was the executive leader of a charter school, I believed the classroom could still give me some access to movement—stepping away from theory alone and intentionally confronting issues of race and class (even if only moderately).

These two realizations lead me to the last, and most important, revelation I have gleaned from this unreturned season in my life. I am a leader—not a teacher. And having a teacher's heart, this juxtaposition of leadership and teaching (as though they are mutually exclusive) is cringy. But this tension is what is at the heart of my third breakthrough in the unreturned. While I have always known that (above all titles) I ultimately am a change agent, my successful (and immensely pleasurable) track record as a teacher made me think that teaching was my exclusive blueprint for change. But (and yes, there is a but), teaching does not embody the deep core of my gift as it does not embody my deepest wiring for movement. I have a keen sensitivity to the social-structural world and no matter what I do, this sensitivity will not be ignored or out-reasoned. I am aware of power points and fault lines as well as actors, agendas, tools, strategies, and systems of power—all of which work together to create and/or prohibit movement work. Not only am I gifted in seeing power at the microscopic level, I am wired to take action (movement).

Most teachers (but certainly not all) float as a way of moving. In other words, the organization moves (as in disrupts or maintains), and teachers, much like the students they serve, consume and comply. As an executive leader, it would be disingenuous if I said that I do not need my own staff to float to some degree. However, I want them to consume and comply with the mission and the vision. Beyond that, it is my desire to hire people who are also wired as movers—getting on the front line to willfully disrupt and fight the status quo. Whether or not the teachers in the districts I work are wired for fighting and disrupting is not the point in this part of the discussion. (Full disclosure, at the time of this revision, I have moved back into a PWI space for a position reportedly designed to serve students at the margins.) This last realization in the *unreturn* is about my wiring for executive movement—a wiring that goes deeply beyond a moral conviction to move. It is deep within my psyche. It is a programming which I cannot undo. The greatest lesson that the unreturned has shown is that only through executive jurisdiction can I move and promote change in the way I have been wired.

TAKE THREE

The name of my central curriculum is SBC Programming (SBC). It is a secondary program that I have continually built and enhanced since 1991. Through it, core subjects such as social studies, language arts, math, science, art, and technology are integrated so as to give students meaningful and rigorous access into higher order thinking (synthesis, evaluation, and creativity). As a formally trained social scientist, a self-declared social change agent, and a heavily licensed social studies teacher across two states, it should go without saying that the curriculum has a strong social justice and social consciousness flair. In a time in our history where we could all stand to be a little more knowledgeable about effective citizenship and civility, I am proud to report that SBC also offers student development in empathy, compassion, responsibility, personal growth, and advocacy.

As a pragmatic progressive, SBC is my disruption as well as my creativity. I am heart bonded to the work it entails and the work it requires. It is for this reason I am guarded in how I spend my core energy in the *unreturn* space as it needs to be protected for SBC's re-implementation. Reinstituting SBC Programming is my *take three* and although I will not unveil the details, I know that this next phase continues my first school's mission and incorporates specific movement—executive movement—for which I was unaware at that time.

Etymology and Mission

Interestingly, I believe I created SBC when I was five years old. If creativity is an act of the mind, then at age five my curriculum for social change began. I went through childhood imagining ways I (and other children) could act as a change agent and I was forever exploring—probing—ways to understand the problems of the social world. There was a time that I wanted to become a politician (which is what convinced me to go to college when, after my horrible experience with high school, I thought I was through with formal education). I thought politics—as in Capital P—was the way to carry out my ideas for social change. But, my three years of serving as a staff assistant for two political organizations (the Mayor's Office and the United States Department of Education) told me that my vision for change agentry could not be realized as a politician.

So I thought to share with other children my passion for change in the social world and equip them with the tools (including imagination and creativity) so they could engage in their own brand of change agentry. And for the most part, acting as a social studies teacher (also being asked to teach reading, language arts, and even religion) gave me the platform to do just that—engage students in social change—in however they understood the problem and imagined their own solutions.

All that work of social change was pushed into second place when I entered into school leadership. Sure, my curriculum (in which the school I founded was born and then the school I inherited was reformed) brought social change into my work as the executive director. But, I got so weighed down with maintaining day-to-day operations that I could not truly do the work of social change. That is, I could not really change the systems that prohibited student learning. I have spent the past five years rethinking the intersections of education and change agentry and I finally now know (which I probably knew back when I was going through teacher training) that my mission to liberate and galvanize students for social change needs an agency (not a school)—one that can equip students with all the literacies (traditional and non-traditional) for achievement that can cause change (production, prosperity, and the promotion of growth).

The Pivot

In short, I have successfully instituted SBC at two schools (one in which I designed and founded and one in which I inherited). I have also earned a master's degree in administrative and instructional leadership where my thesis focused on the tenets of successful schooling. Finally, I earned a PhD where my dissertation transcended "schooling" and focused on the tenets of successful learning as relating to power, class, and race. Through it all, I have more of a macro understanding and charge to the curriculum than I did when it was first formed.

Initially, the curriculum had a micro-level mission assuming that the real work of learning (and disruption) was about students. I felt students had been disenfranchised from the learning process and their lived realities needed to be made relevant in the classroom– in the curricular choices that were selected and in the delivery of instruction in which they received. I assumed with those changes (making sure instruction was culturally relevant to their lived experiences), social change could occur. This focus on students and instruction is what I now call a micro-based treatment to the work as it does not acknowledge the macro—the social structural conditions that insidiously influence learning and development.

It was one of my student leaders from my first school who actually woke me up from my micro-based slumber. Sure, my doctoral degree gave me a macro lens to the social world; however, it was this student, in her frustration with me, who showed me the practical limitations of a micro-focused treatment of the curriculum. I have talked about her before across other platforms. Specifically in the book, *Empowerment Starts Here* (Dye, 2012), I called her *Lisa* and talked about the essential leadership role she played in helping me manage the school. But, on my podcast, "Empowerment Starts Here," I talked about her disappointment with me—a disappointment critical for a conversation about *take three*.

Lisa said I had empowered them (she and her classmates) for a world that did not want them empowered. And while her words and her disappointment hit me like a gut punch, I realized she was absolutely right. Focusing on curriculum alone (even a culturally responsive curriculum) did not change the world's oppressive treatment towards them. It simply positioned them in that world with contemporary skills all while leaving them void of skills needed to fight for and protect their own humanity.

The Critical

One of the strengths of SBC is that it truly gives students traditional and non-traditional skills. And while critical skills (the ones *Lisa* and her classmate needed) are a branch of non-traditional skills, they require their own distinction as they are the skills that will specifically focus on oppression. Traditional elementary and secondary skills (such as reading, writing and computation) help students moderately maneuver through the demands of social living. Non-traditional elementary and secondary skills (such as creative problem solving, innovation, and management) help students to competitively maneuver through the demands of social living.

However, critical skills (such as locating and exposing hidden agendas, code-switching, and political coalition building) help students to be whole and fully human in a social world that is designed to keep them in a subhuman (second class) state.

In my Empowerment Framework, I center all these skills within a context of power. Power building (the traditional route to power), power-sharing (the non-traditional route to power), and power resisting (the critical route to power) are all necessary to thrive in the social world. *Lisa* helped me because she brought into focus the limitations of skill development without understanding how the social world consistently uses power. Without a lens for macro-related power, we suffocate and stress students who go out in the world with basic literacies or even those literacies afforded to them by a true culturally relevant curriculum (assuming they will have teachers who can stand the consequences of truly teaching in a way that is culturally relevant). In addition, we indirectly pressure them to succumb to learning and knowing that makes them only suited for a life of compliance and consumption—serving as a continuous cog in an oppressive infrastructure.

The only way students can be groomed and positioned to confront systems of oppression is to give them critical literacies for social change—a change that truly disrupts the margins in which they have been placed. This change goes beyond the margins that relate to students as learners and includes those that relate to them as women, disabled, and immigrants; as well as religious, language, cognitive, racial and sexual minorities. This is what my curriculum at the next level aims to do. Encouraging them to define their own political agenda, they will learn critical literacies right alongside the traditional and non-traditional literacies needed for the real world in which they will live—in all, allowing them to be successful, competitive, and fully human.

At the time of my last revision to this text, there is a nationwide conversation about critical race theory in education. While I do not connect pragmatic progressivism to critical race theory, the tenets are here all the same. Critical race theory in education is about addressing the invisible structures that impede the justice and humanity of learners at the margins. Those who are upset with the influence of critical race theory are benefactors of those structures. Giving these structures visibility threatens the benefits that exist when they are invisible. I am set to compile a collection of essays I have written on the *critical* into a book; however, the topic is being mentioned in this text to acknowledge that there is a national conversation—a conversation that will no doubt impact the pragmatic progressive's ability to really take on the work. No student who is structurally in the margins of society should be taught in the absence of tenets that will help him to succeed, compete, and be fully human.

WHAT TAKE THREE IS NOT (A CRITIQUE)

I want to acknowledge that culturally relevant teaching, an already active movement in schools, also embraces tenets of critical race theory. You can especially see its influence when Ladson-Billings (2009) briefly talks about it as a pedagogy of opposition. As a pedagogy of opposition, she argues that teachers must challenge (disrupt) the structures that prevent learning—even when those structures are mandates of the job. Most people who champion culturally relevant teaching do so without acknowledging the oppositional work it requires. They do so without acknowledging the harm that the profession at times enacts on learners. This oblivion is what my *take three* is not. As a result, and with a great deal of trepidation, I want to challenge the practice because of this under-pronounced position on opposition. Its low-visibility (if at all) is what prevents culturally relevant teaching from reaching its full potential. It is the full potential for which I am aiming in my *take three* and it is the full potential that I believe is at the heart of the pragmatic progressive.

In short, the problem with culturally relevant teaching, as I talk in more detail and clarity in my 300(plus) page dissertation, is that it challenges the process of instruction without challenging the outcomes of instruction. Through a community-orientated research approach, Gloria Ladson-Billings invited mothers to define the scope of good teaching. Because of their input (also with the input of her teacher informants), good teaching was defined by three outcomes: academic achievement, cultural competencies, and critical consciousness. While these outcomes are the genius to culturally relevant teaching, the work of trying to accommodate those outcomes without challenging the system by which those outcomes would be measured was short-sighted. Teachers across the country trying to implement culturally relevant teaching are faced with the challenge of teaching for those outcomes all while having to face employment (and evaluation) outcomes that are often antithetical to the outcomes embedded within culturally relevant teaching.

Measurements such as standardized test scores, attendance, discipline records, and college admission rates, while fine and good, are all byproducts of an oppressive structure where power holders do very little to disrupt the power distribution that maintains their power. For example (as discussed in Chapter 2), standardized tests are designed to sort, separate, and rank students. No matter how students grow, in route to closing the "achievement gap," the test will be updated so as to continue to show a ranking. Even in spaces where students of color outperform their White counterparts, our school ethos does very little to recognize the value, and embedded power, that this area of knowing offers.

Another measurement of culturally relevant teaching that while valid (particularly as relating to the mother-informants in Ladson-Billings's [2009] research) still needs to be interrogated is college enrollment. College enrollment is an important part of empowerment, but it, statistically speaking, plays a very small role in the work of empowerment. The best way to tackle the limitations that college enrollment has on the empowerment of students is looking at the socioeconomic conditions of African-American women. Black women in the United States are the most college educated as a demographic collective. Yet, they remain to be the least paid, the least represented in political office, and the most at risk for health disparities, predatory lending, and imprisonment in the prison industrial complex system. I do not write these outcomes as a way of discrediting college enrollment. I write them to suggest that there are additional outcomes (such as production, prosperity, and the promotion of growth) to be considered when measuring educational achievement and attainment.

My *take three* wants to get students "to produce, to prosper, and to promote growth" in an environment that will not be tied down to artificial constructs of achievement that ultimately are oppressive. It will be oppositional to the forces that harm and committed to equipping students with critical literacies for the invisible. It will pursue measurements that capture the real work of liberation and not measurements that continue to be defined and engineered by the benefactors of oppression.

CLOSING THOUGHTS

I started this book with a dedication to three women who influenced my movement from being a progressive educator to being a pragmatic progressive educator. This movement has been about the real demands of living in the social world. I often think progressive educators (not all of them of course) are more focused on the world as it should be and not on the world as it is. As a result, they do not—as I was accused by *Lisa* (the student leader discussed earlier in this chapter)—give an adequate education for students who depend on it as an equalizer.

This is the final thought I want to share as I close. Education has utility and depending on who it serves will depend on what we should do with it. Students in the margins are capable of progressive style learning, where they have freedom, agency, and dignity; and, where they are able to think in abstraction, produce new knowledge and considerations, lead others, and solve complex problems. What they also need as they are learning these complex maneuvers is a learning environment that acknowledges the stress and trauma of living in the margins and provides them with a type of instructional safety.

People are often confused by my practice because on one level, I can have a high level of control. As attributed to many African-American educators, I will exact what I expect. This exacting is called being a warm demander. Gloria Ladson-Billings talked about it in her book, *Dream Keepers*, and mentioned the value of teachers caring enough (believing enough) about their students to demand—to accept nothing less than success. When visitors get beyond the control I have in the room, where failure is one choice not allowed (which can be antithetical to a pure progressive educational agenda), they will see students not only thriving in their agency for higher-order thinking but relishing in it as well. As a pragmatic progressive, I have a macro agenda that extends beyond the individual student. My agenda is for the collective, and the individual student is a critical piece in the advancement of that whole. As a result, I will not allow students to squander their time to satisfy a social narrative that limits them to a permanent underclass. This non-negotiable is what Gloria Ladson-Billings, Marva Collins, and Lisa Delpit taught me in my beginning years as a progressive educator. They demanded that I attend to the social context of students' lived reality and the political context of the schools and communities that house and serve them.

In my first book, *Empowerment Starts Here* (Dye, 2012), and my dissertation, *The Phenomenon of Student Powerlessness* (Dye, 2014), I give recognition to theorists who informed my practice as a progressive. However, I realize that I do not really do so in this text. So before closing, let me give more space to John Dewey and Parker Palmer as two of my progressive education informants. Through them, I learned about education as a utility and studentship as a condition of heart and soul. But, their impact on my thinking pales in contrast to the impact of Delpit, Collins, and Ladson-Billings. Because of these three women, I can take the work of Dewey and Palmer to the margins. In all, I am positioned to move forward to confront and disrupt education systems that were built in tandem with forces that cause harm.

I am thankful for my exposure to these women as they validated an intuitive part of me that had to suffer alone in a progressive environment. While a progressive educational approach is grounded in many of the values I hold, it is missing some tenets students need to thrive. On the other hand, traditional environments attend to some of the pieces progressive spaces disregard. In all however, my ultimate passion as an educator leans progressive—being able to lift students up to be agents of transformation so they can contend with the forces (social, cultural, interpersonal, and/or intrapersonal) that prohibit their transcendence.

TO THE EMERGING PRAGMATIC PROGRESSIVE

Regardless of your entry into the practice, whether your start is progressive or traditional, there will be tension points to the application of pragmatic progressivism as it is an applied theory in the margins. As I bring closure to this text, I want to tell you more about the tension points and to equip you with strategies to stay the course. I will assume that you found your way to this book (and remained) because the tenets within resonate with your core orientation toward education and its relationship to the world. Just as followers of Ladson-Billings's work (culturally relevant teaching) have experienced conflict between the theory and the application, I am not naïve to believe that pragmatic progressivism will be any easier. I want to posit, however, that the pragmatic progressive might be even more difficult to implement not only because it is a hybrid of polarizing philosophies but because it is an *applied* construct.

In Chapters 2 and 3 of this text, I provided concrete considerations of pragmatic progressivism as related to practice. While Chapter 2 is framed as a political shift, I talk about specific methods such as skill (and concept) isolation, measuring, reporting, and accountability. Then in Chapter 3, I talk about specific strategies to use as key components to instruction. All of it together can feel like a prescription, which is what many culturally responsive practitioners try to avoid… and rightfully so. They believe that once you provide a prescription, it prevents practitioners from creatively moving and adjusting to meet the needs of their learners.

I will be the first to argue that prescriptions in this book can prohibit the effectiveness of pragmatic progressives. However, I stand firm that having no prescription can stifle us as well. I see prescriptions as starting points. They are like a recipe that was handed down to you from your grandmother's grandmother. Each time that recipe is passed along, there is a slight change to meet the desired taste of those who will eat the dish in its present day context. For example, I was the one to start cooking turnip and mustard greens with smoked turkey tails. My grandmother and her grandmother cooked them with smoked ham hocks. I made the change, going from ham hocks to turkey tails because I gave up pork almost thirty years ago. This past Christmas, out of all the family meals that occurred in our large family, no one cooked with the pork. Every household (and yes, every household had turnip and mustards), the greens were cooked with turkey meat. With the goal of serving a delicious, but healthy, pot of greens, the original recipe was modified. In order for the modification to occur, there ultimately needed to be a start... a recipe... a prescription.

Pragmatic progressives can embrace prescriptions as starts so they too can be effective. Being effective in the work of freedom, dignity, and change—that is the ultimate aim.

In saying this, I want to assert that I hold more to the philosophy of the pragmatic progressive than the prescription. As more fully discussed in Chapter 4, pragmatic progressivism is about promoting ideals of liberation and prosperity all while recognizing a social world that is inherently oppressive—so much so that tools touted as champions of freedom ultimately, and insidiously, deny students of their dignity and humanity. The pragmatic progressive must teach in a way that exposes the insidious nature of traditional education all while equipping students with the literacies it generates.

This balance between disruption and extraction is akin to Melissa Harris Perry's (a political scientist who I deeply admire) argument that surviving and thriving in an oppressive world requires that we both resist and accommodate. The degree to which we do either speaks to our own brand of intolerance (or tolerance for that matter) and, above all else, our end game. The end game of the pragmatic progress is not pragmatic progressivism (like the end game to progressive education is not—or should not— be progressivism). The end game is what the pragmatic progressive aims to achieve (again, not what he aims to do). If we aim to promote the liberty, dignity, wholeness, and advancement of our learners, we will do whatever it takes—resistance *and* accommodation—to get there.

This is the final reminder I want to make as I close the text. The pragmatic progressive is a by-any-means-necessary practitioner with one specific goal in mind for the learner. The outcome does not change but the methods can change... and should!! In a climate that is more prone to the rhetoric of ideals, more so than the application of those ideals, the pragmatic progressive is a dual resister—resisting the oppression of disadvantaged learners and resisting feel good rhetoric that has no measurable application. The pragmatic progressive is an applied philosophy that is committed to an outcome. Yes, it offers a prescription but truthfully, it is very comfortable with denouncing and tossing out that prescription if (and as) it interferes with the ultimate objective.

In saying all of this, I invite practitioners reading this book to throw everything I have said out the window if it, on any level, interferes with the true mission of pragmatic progressivism. This is an applied practice. Make it work by any means necessary and be a true part of the change we want to see in the world.

Good luck!!

REFERENCE LIST

Chappell, B. (2017, June 22). Census finds a more diverse America, as Whites lag growth. *National Public Radio*. Retrieved from https://www.npr.org/sections/thetwo-way/2017/06/22/533926978/census-finds-a-more-diverse-america-as-whites-lag-growth

Delpit, L. (1995). *Other people's children: Cultural conflict in the classroom*. New York, NY: The New Press.

Dye, A. (2012).*Empowerment starts here: Seven principles to empowering urban youth*. Lanham, MD: Rowman and Littlefield.

Dye, A. (Host). (2017-present). *Empowerment starts here* [Audiopodcast]. PBS Development, LLC. https://empowermentstartshere.net/the-eshpodcast

Dye, A. Y. (2014). The phenomenon of student powerlessness and student achievement: An instrumental multi-case student on the practices of three teachers identified as successfully serving low-income African American students (Doctoral Dissertation). Capella University. Retrieved from ProQuest Dissertations and Theses database.

Ladson-Billings, G. (2009). The d*reamkeepers: Successful teachers of African American children* (2nd ed). San Francisco, CA: Jossey-Bass Publishers.

Willie, C. (2001). The contextual effects of socioeconomic status on student achievement test scores by race. *Urban Education*. Retrieved from http:///uex.sagepub.com/content/36/4/461

EduMatch

PUBLISHING

eloveate

dive deep, vibe high, radiate love

nicole miles

Printed in the United States of America

Published in Hellertown, PA

Library of Congress Control Number 2023916568

ISBN 978-1-958711-73-6

For more information or to place bulk orders, contact the author at eloveation.nation@gmail.com or the publisher at Jennifer@BrightCommunications.net.

To my younger self

This book contains the basics of all that I needed to know but wasn't taught. So, here you go, honey. You did such a good job discovering it on your own.

Life is tricky. Here's a manual to help you.

contents

introduction

On the day of our birth, we all experience a
separation. As we are separated from our mothers, the
source of our existence, our spirits also seem to separate from the divine source as they enter the material
and dense plane of Earth. Life is a journey back to
wholeness, so we can claim union once again with
that divine source and feel the embrace of love around
us at all times, releasing any idea of separation. This
union reconnects us to the flow of truth, which guides
our growth and well-being. As we allow ourselves to
be held in the loving gaze and knowing hands of this
higher aspect of us, we awaken to the light within us
and begin to feel at one with the divine.

In the concise chapters of this book, you will learn
how to reclaim the connection to your divinity and
begin to heal the separation you experienced at birth.
The light you are has never dimmed, but it has been

obscured by a world designed to challenge you. This book is your starter manual to peeling back the layers of obscurity and rising to a new way of being.

I call this process "eloveation." No, I didn't spell it wrong. Yes, it is pronounced almost exactly the same as "elevation." But spelling counts. And the fact that LOVE is inserted into the middle of a word that means "the height of" matters. Rising up with LOVE as the center force—that matters. Love is always the answer. It is the driving force of creation, the language of God.

So yeah, eloveation is a word now. I didn't come up with it; it was given to me, channeled as I sketched one day. The word, the meaning, and the three facets to change the world (dive deep, vibe high, radiate love) are the formula that you will come back to over and over again. Along with my symbol of a deep sea, a high mountain, and a heart radiating love—all of that came from God.

If I could add eloveation to the official dictionaries of the world, it would be entered as:

Pronunciation: el-ov-ay-shun

Definition: (n) eloveation: the process of rising to a higher vibration through healing oneself and remembering one's innate divinity; rising up, becoming enlightened, ascending, living as more light

(v) eloveate: Pronounced: el-ov-ate

To deeply dive into oneself to heal the illusions of separation, which automatically raises one's vibration, which results in having a hugely open, wise, and radiant heart of love, which magnetizes in a life of love.

The simple words spoken through these pages will be an initiation to the divine truths you'll encounter about your true nature as you embark on the deeper journey of self-knowing. These brief chapters act as portals for you to enter the path of self-awareness. The simple, channeled wisdom reveals things we aren't taught but really need to know to live fulfilling lives. These truths are ancient, built into our DNA, part of our divine heritage, and ready for you to embrace.

You will find the journey of self-discovery is like a set of Russian stacking dolls: The first shell opens to reveal another and then another and another. Each time you open a new layer, more tools will be revealed to you. You'll continue this unshelling until you get, at last, to a solid core, the understanding of who you are, meeting the most intact version of you. This is the one who knows itself and cannot be split apart. This version of you is true, pure, rich, unique, and whole. It is God, embodied. It is the blessed state of self-knowing and oneness that can never be taken from you. Once you know, you know.

As you read, hear the voice of your divine Creator, who birthed the dream of you ages ago, speaking words of truth to you. Feel yourself welcomed into the arms of the Divine, the one who loves unconditionally and sees all. These are the truths you were meant to live by, the truths of who you are, despite what your experience in the world has led you to believe.

By picking up this book, you are ready to release any deception you might have that you are less than divine perfection.

Get ready to eloveate!

1
you are magic

There is a magical, unseen force in this universe. It is in the energy of creation and destruction, in the movement of molecules, in the power of magnetism, in the forces of nature. This magical force makes seasons change, lightning flash, and tides rise and fall. You, as a living breathing part of nature, are made from and of this magic. The magical, source energy of our universe has created the most beautiful and breathtaking experiences and places, and it created you.

You are both magic and magician, a creator of your own life, using creativity and the ability to impress upon the canvas of existence your will. You are not separate from this magic force. It lives inside of you. This magic is not a talent bestowed upon the most elite few. It is the way of the universe. It is for all and every being. It begins within the cosmic mind, a spark of energetic creation.

While you might not yet agree that you are the magic described herein, you will soon. It is important that you release the stories told to you and held within you that restrict you as anything less than magical and powerful. You are not a passive being, not a piece of luggage towed along on a belt. You matter, and you possess all the power you need to create whatever you want. You can, through sheer faith and consistent focus, impress your creative will upon what we call "reality." In fact, you are unconsciously creating your world every minute with every conscious thought and subconscious belief, and you might not even realize it. The past and all you have experienced are not an indicator of your magic. Your magic is part of who you are. It lives inside your DNA, in the spaces that are unnamed.

This ability to create based on what you emit is an amazing thing to discover. It is both empowering and humbling to learn this. It is empowering because we realize we have much more control of what we experience than we have been led to believe. It is humbling because we begin to see how we have created our world up to this point, and once we do, we realize we are responsible for it all. We see our seamless connection to everything we perceive.

Creation is an unbiased deal, so it equally includes both the things we do and do not want, a bit of a tug-of-war between all that you want and all that you fear, between desire and dread. This process of creating is occurring constantly, even when you aren't aware and aren't trying. It happens when you take in the world around you and react to it. It happens with your every thought, emotion, and action. It involves your subconscious agreements in each moment regarding what is true and to what you give energy through agreements and attention.

This is massively important to understand and grasp if you are to truly direct your life with the unfolding you desire. Mastering your creation means reclaiming your magician status and having constant awareness of your thoughts and feelings. This means making really hard choices. It means living in the now every second with careful self-awareness and discipline.

Often being a magical creator means having such a carefully honed technology for checking in with yourself and feeling into your surroundings that you can tune yourself to just the right frequency for just the right experiences. It involves developing the skill of sensing each aspect of "reality" to determine if it fits into the overall scheme of what you desire and then using your innate tech to modify it. It also means you take the power you hold as a magician seriously—to use this technology with discernment and the touch of pure intention. It's a mighty skill indeed. No wonder this is not something taught to us!

Claiming and using this magic is intricate. Living as a magician requires both conscious self-control and faith as big as mountains, faith that you truly can create absolutely anything. Most notably, it means being vigilant and selective about your intake and outflow of energy. That begins with paying attention, which requires significantly slowing down from the pace of the surrounding world of distractions.

It means getting in touch with yourself in deeply honest ways and truly tuning into the inner world of YOU. This means spending quiet, uninterrupted time with yourself. One of the major skills you develop in this alone, quiet time is the ability to know your own energy, apart from the influence of others. This allows you to become familiar with your boundaries and preferences. Once you know yourself and how you feel in your own heart and mind and body, learning your own signature, you become more proficient in discerning energy and noticing the way thoughts and actions impact you. You also learn what is yours and what is not.

The reward for this deep work is grand. Once you learn to discern energy and get to know yourself intimately, you will begin to master your self-awareness, and you will be able to identify what is most desirable to you, setting yourself solidly in the resonance of YOU.

Staying in this strong resonance of YOU emits a signal. The longer you can stay in the resonance of YOU, the more powerfully you emit, like a lighthouse. The light frequency of YOU that you emit becomes an actual energetic note, a tone that is uniquely encoded. The universe receives this frequency and will line up all the tools, circumstances, and people to help you accomplish your desires if you are able to maintain the fertility of your desire, the consistency of your tone. Continue to stay in the strong YOU, keeping the tone of your desires clear, open, and centered in your powerful heart. You will become a beacon of YOUness and attract into your life the experiences that align with your resonance.

Staying in a powerful resonance of YOUness can be quite a challenge without a trained mind. Unless you have grown up in nirvana, unscathed by society and unencumbered by beliefs and agreements of others and institutions, you likely accumulated "stuff" in your mind and body that doesn't support your desires. This "stuff" consists mostly of negative and limiting beliefs and will actually work behind the scenes, on a subconscious level, to create a reality that opposes the one you're trying to consciously create.

Clearing the limiting belief systems that pull you away from your desires requires a defragmenting of your system. It requires an unlearning of all that is in contrast to what you know to be your most wonderful, fulfilled life. You need to shut down the systems in the subconscious that are negatively impacting your will in order to empower your conscious desires to be the dominant creative team in charge. Essentially, you need to sort out the junk mail of your brain and heart on a daily basis and not allow anything to remain that doesn't align with your highest truth. This can be tricky because life is an accumulation of learning what "reality" is like. Our accumulated concepts of reality create belief systems that get stored and then influence our present thoughts and resonance.

Let's take money as an example of accumulated subconscious belief systems that might be affecting your current resonance. What are your beliefs about money? How do you relate to money? What is that relationship like for you? Has it always been that way? The families we grow up in, the communities in which we live, where we fit into the socioeconomic hierarchy, and the experiences we have at an early age with the flow of money and the beliefs about what it symbolizes and how it works all contribute to deep beliefs about it. Later in life, we might have problems rooted in not having enough money or having plenty and struggling with how that adds to our identity and relational dynamics.

Until we get very clear about these beliefs, we will not be a magnet for what we desire because these subconscious patterns will be running interference. Sometimes these are really, really deep and subtle, and we have to do some extra digging to find the roots. Often life will continue to slam us with struggles until we get the courage to do the necessary digging. We must face the sub—the underneath, hidden, lurking beliefs that are nagging at our abilities to live the way we desire. We must *dive deep* to extract these subconscious patterns that inform most areas of life, including relationships, wellness, and success.

We live in a programmed system that doesn't want you to realize your power, your magic. It's archaic and self-serving. It doesn't want you to know that you are a powerful creator, that you are limitless and magnificent. In the eyes of the system, your living blindly and believing that life is *happening to you,* that you have little power to direct it, makes you more controllable, a better pawn.

When you do not know you are magic, you're more likely to buy things, to want things that fill you up and give you temporary feelings of control or being valuable, to numb yourself. You are more likely to obey external authority and feel small and obedient. Living inside this deceptive cloak is the separation from truth that makes you feel limited and powerless. You might feel anxious, depressed, and unwell and need to fill yourself from outside with food and drink and sex and clothes, with cars and trips and stuff.

(How convenient: Stuff makes those other creators rich!)

Living in the false illusion will keep you feeling powerless and empty, and you will long to fill your void with whatever appeals as the solution to your feeling of limitation and lack. This is the never-ending cycle of entrapment that leaves many people feeling empty, anxious, depressed, imprisoned, stale, and lost. The entrapment is why healing and living well are delayed and sometimes elude people for their entire lives.

The actual truth, found only outside of the societal programming we have been raised into, is that your contentment comes from knowing that life is to be self-created and that life is an exploration, a feast of experience, a journey, a process, a creative venture filled with many experiences. When you step outside of the program, outside of the stuff you have taken on, outside of the inaccurate beliefs about who you are and what you are capable of, outside of the duality of good or bad, worthy or unworthy, you step into the truth that you are indeed magic.

Once you begin the journey inward, to the truth of yourself and your energy, to the fact that most of what was running your life was an illusion, you come to a point of union with yourself. You are the very essence of God / the Divine / the universe / the magician. Welcome home!

Pulling yourself outside of the program takes a spark of magic. Some call it an awakening because you are waking up from an illusion, a bad dream of sorts, to the truth. Often awakening comes via trauma, when the false illusory world you bought into crumbles in your hands. This often happens when a person loses a loved one or a job or encounters a major life change. When you are faced with a crumbling past, a new space opens for living as a magician. When the veil of illusion falls away, you can begin realizing your truth. During awakening, at the highest peaks of truth that one can glimpse, you actually meet your inner magic/God/divinity.

For me, the feeling of awakening was akin to the feeling I felt when I was about to give birth to my first baby. It was new and terrifying at first. I couldn't use anything tangible to escape its inevitability. I felt massive pain and discomfort, and I was realizing that a phase of my life was ending. But I was honored and excited as much as I was terrified. When the fear fell away, God was there smiling at me, gesturing me inward, and I came face-to-face with creation, divine love, God's essence.

Discovering that something beautiful was wanting me to explore deeper, to go into a new truth, was rooted in so much love. It was a life-changing feeling. It was like standing at God's doorstep and ringing the door-bell. For me, time stood still, and the immense feeling of magic in all its wonder came rushing through me. It was both terrifying and thrilling. It felt like an opening into something vast and infinite while everything around me was crumbling.

Having limitlessness feels like a free fall, like floating in the wide-open sea. My concept of myself had been miniscule, but in that moment of quiet in between pains—and in similar moments since—the contrast of truth has been so drastic. The pain revealed the relief.

When we finally open up to it, the truth of our divinity, to knowing we are magic, is so expansive the mind never returns to its prior state. In the letting go, into the wide-open infinity of your magic, you will find an inconceivable new recalibration. And it will be terrifying—but rewarding.

Awakening is hard. It is uncharted territory where there is a discovery of big and small lies, misconceptions, and a revisiting of old traumas. It requires us to clear out and rebuild the entire concept of reality. The deep dive is a lot of work. It involves acceptance of things we might not enjoy and acknowledgment of a world that has been bent to pieces. But as the space inside of us grows, more light comes in, and in that light, we are reconnected to magic, to source, to the divine within.

As you begin to familiarize with the magician within, you gain understanding of the program you have been living inside. The program the world is running on is a creation that has built over time and continues to have steam in the direction of itself, like an object on a trajectory with inertia. It is built through group consciousness and agreement of the masses. It's up to you to awaken from this hive-mind creation and see it for the trapping it is, then choose to create your own reality with your own magic.

The invitation to wake up to this truth in this lifetime is here. It's now. It's time to start the adventure of clearing your path—so you can create your best reality.

The designing of a new way of life here on Earth begins with you. You accumulate a lot of information about the world around you. You begin to feel uncomfortable with it. You wake up to how misaligned that information is with the deeper sense of truth inside of you, and you begin the process of cleaning up and then creating from a new conceptualized sense of your true power, from divine inspiration. This is alchemy, magic, and transformation.

As you move through the process of dissolution and recreation, you can repeatedly say no to what was and yes to what you prefer. Everything you do is a vote for the old way or a vote for your aligned, divinely inspired way of life. The vote is for entrapment or creation, outside programming or inner inspiration. Getting quiet and developing your sense of inner knowing is key.

Everything that ever was and ever will be came from creation, from magic. Every creation was backed by a will, an inspiration, a spark, for it to come into existence and be witnessed. This will, which is a concentration of focused creative energy, lives inside of you. Your greatest dreams will become a reality in some fashion if there is enough positive focus to move them through the levels of vibration, or vibrancy—as long as there is no resistance keeping them from manifesting. Extracting the blockages opens the flow of creative energy.

For a moment, envision an image that begins as foggy, dreamy, and far away. Now steadily apply more focus, appreciation, and attention to it, with strong awareness of it and its details. See how it becomes more vibrant, more focused, and powerfully anchored in what we call reality. This is how you embody your role as a magician, as a manifestor of what you desire. Dream it, feel it, see it, love it. Hold it gently, with an open hand. Apply patience and faith and hold it as an absolute. Eliminate any form of resistance so your magic can bring forth everything and anything you wish to create. Practice your magic and keep track of it. Notice your progress. Always clear the old, lower data that is not aligned with love and fosters fear. Allow yourself to be magic, magician, creator.

2
tuning in to you mindfully

In chapter one, we established that you are the magician, the one creating your own life story and experiences. It is important to understand the balance of power in this creation process. In this thing we call reality, there are many, many magicians, each with their own creative abilities and awareness of these capabilities. Each of these magicians is imprinting their desires onto the grid of "reality." Although you do not solely control this reality, you do get a say via what you imprint.

You start with controlling your portion of the pie. You learn how to master yourself so that you have a strong, pure tool with which to imprint. You become a clear, concentrated beacon so that your desires have momentum and a strong resonance. Rather than living on autopilot, unaware of what you are creating, weakly surviving inside of the programming of others, far from your own truth, you become a manifestor, generating your own signature, poetic essence of your most fulfilling creations.

So how does one become this clear and concentrated beacon? This is where mindfulness comes into play. This is a tool for self-mastery. Mindfulness practices allow you to become a slow, still witness. Mindfulness practices take your attention from the "out there" of the external world and bring you to the "in here, right now, at this exact moment" of your own internal world. The right here, exact present moment, just this one inhale, is the only thing that is true. The past, even one second ago, is a memory, and the future has not yet been created.

This one moment in time is where you can settle into stillness and clarity. This is how you connect to your essence. Rather than the stories of the ego, the regrets, the anxieties, the striving, you connect to the essence of your being. This is how you get to know you as a unique essence. Your right now, right here, present moment of being is an important address within time and space.

The present is a present. If you are seeking connection with the divine source, that spark of magic, it is in this right here, right now time and space that you find it. You just have to be ready for the connection. Mindfulness brings you to the present so the wisdom of the universe can find you and fill you with magic. Staying present is like staying home to receive the package. It is essential to have your whole self together and be at ease in order to receive the magic. It is also the place where you hold resonance for what you desire— feeling it, seeing it, nurturing the essence of it until it becomes manifest.

Mindfulness also helps you understand the impact of your thoughts and patterns and that you are not the actual thoughts and patterns themselves. By knowing your thoughts and how they are affecting your reality, you can change them and select a new direction. You do this by choosing to create new thoughts and patterns. The reprogramming of your mind leads to a change in your experience. Spending even one moment of mindful pause pays huge dividends in your capacity to know yourself and become a discerning creator.

With an awareness of the mind, you regain control of your life in a way greater than you were taught to believe possible. You begin to consciously question your habitual beliefs and directions of the mind. You become familiar with the ego, as you compassionately witness its desire to try to protect you, its ancient programming delivering doubt and fear to you, inad-vertently keeping you both safe and imprisoned. With your mindful awareness of the self, you begin to reject the influence of the outside world and the old, habitual, untrue belief systems. You start to notice the sensations in your energy field that feel "off" because you slow down and begin paying attention in this way.

The biggest challenge in practicing mindfulness, and ultimately meditation, is quieting the mind and releasing the powerful grip that old ways seem to have on us. Sometimes the chaos of the mind is overwhelming, and finding a starting point seems impossible. There will be the sensation of monkeys and mice chattering about inside your mind and in your surroundings to derail you. They are there because we believe we need to be filled all the time, processing information as a means of survival. Distractions and chaos have been the main program in the human mind. Humans have evolved to hold a capacity for information and an ability to quickly shift focus. This developed in a world of feeling unsafe, as a survival mechanism.

Mindfulness allows you to identify how you function within the chaos by pausing, slowing, and checking in on how you feel. What are the sensations in your body? Is there tension in any joints or muscles? Are there jittery parts? Is there tiredness or contraction? Are you breathing fast or slow? With what are you identifying right now?

Using mindfulness to check in with bodily cues can inform you of the underlying dynamics and how you are navigating them. Find safety in the quiet. Feel it as a welcome reprieve from the circus of an unconscious program.

Mindfulness practices enable you to metaphorically take your own temperature by stopping and checking on yourself. This looks like taking a breath, closing your eyes, and asking, "How am I? What am I experiencing? Where do I feel it most?" With practice, you learn to carefully and quickly tune into yourself to get a reading on how you are *being*.

Mindfulness can be developed into a sort of medicinal salve for healing unhealthy patterns. It might mean labeling or identifying the distracting stories or beliefs that are running the sabotage program inside of you. Witnessing them takes away their power over you. You might pause to say, "I see there is nervousness in my belly. I am worried I will fail. I am buying into the belief that I am not enough, which I know is untrue. This is actually the voice of my mother, not my higher self. This is an old program, and I am now releasing myself from the binding of it and stepping into my truth. My truth is that I was, am, and will always be enough, simply because I was created and I am a piece of divinity."

After you learn this process of becoming aware of yourself, you can get in touch with the inner chatter and gauge your beliefs and thoughts. Ask yourself how you are feeling, and why. Learn to question the truth of a situation and gain perspective. By taking the pause, you stop the flow of panic and the desire to react. In the pause, you breathe and gain space between the chaos and the possible solutions. Often, after a few breaths, the pattern is broken, and you are liberated into a sense of spaciousness in which you can freely breathe and become open to new opportunities to experience the situation differently and with a better outcome. Taking a mindful detour can be medicinal, rerouting us onto a better course of action and changing our programmed behavioral patterns .

Mindful practice allows you to move from instinctual fight, flight, or freeze to calm, which brings healing and reprogramming to you. It also reprograms you from living in a mimic pattern of what has been to a creative pattern of what will be—designing your life based on your preference and will, taking you out of the known rut and putting you on a new path.

There is a defining element of mindfulness that is liberating, too. You begin to ask yourself if you are falling into the stories of the past and staying there too long or jumping ahead with worry over the future, drowning in anxious energy. You liberate your "right here" self into ease by noticing where you are in time and space and how it is making you feel. This creates an intimacy with the deeper aspects of your soul's essence.

With practice, you learn how to quiet the chatter, how to find a bit of peace. Your mind will run less on the old autopilot mode (chaos) and more on your newly programmed mode (clarity). Using techniques that pull you out of chaos and into clarity actually rewires your brain. Rewiring lets you sidestep the nonsense that is trying to keep you in ego and old patterns. This is the key to becoming a creator of what you desire, an on-purpose creator instead of one who is *unconsciously* creating life.

Noticing the voice who is leading the stories of the mind is key. Is the thought you're dancing around coming from a place of fear or love? My guess is that if you get caught in the vortex of negative thoughts or beliefs, it is coming from fear, which comes not from God and love, but from the limiting ego. Simply noticing that the story is one of fear and not love can be enough to make you jump from the track of destruction to the path of freedom.

The outside world is designed to keep you scared, lonely, and out of union with yourself. It is loud and busy on purpose. Learn to know your thoughts. But always remember that *you* are not *your thoughts*. Often, your thoughts are a soundtrack that plays automatically and is the accumulation of the things you have absorbed and believed to be true from the world around you. The words you hear inside are the voices of your parents, teachers, friends, and classmates or messages from TV, movies, social media, and music.

The impulses of the autopilot program are often triggers from people and situations in your environment. Pausing frequently to breathe and question your current state and mindset is the first and simplest step to living as a conscious creator. Simply pause and question.

How have we not learned this stuff? We experience years of mandated education, and we often follow that with years of higher education or training, yet we need to be reminded to go within. Seems strange, no? School systems teach you to learn many things about the world around you, plenty of what they claim the human story is all about historically as well as the scientific and mathematical concepts by which the world is constructed, but they rarely teach you to know yourself. This seems like learning about the road, trees, signs, and stop lights—without knowing how to drive the car.

You must learn who you are inside. It is time to love all the aspects of yourself and live in your own truth, not the truth of people around you. It is time to get to know yourself intimately. The awakening is a time of learning about yourself and the false world around you.

Throughout your childhood, you were being programmed for survival, often doing what you needed to do to be cared for, loved, and protected. You needed acceptance to be part of the caregivers' world of food, shelter, and protection that is required as a small mammal on Earth. You learned about the world around you and how to be in it in a successful way as a survivor.

However, a lot of that story was fictitious, things you pieced together as seeming truth. As a small human with a developing brain in a reality where outside programming is powerful, you naturally created some limiting beliefs about yourself and the world around you. This is what you get to unlearn in your awakening. You also get to learn "you" from a much more loving and less vulnerable point of awareness.

Learning you is like learning how to use a car's navigation. It isn't about memorizing the coordinates. It is about driving with a plan and allowing the rightness of each step and decision to lead you to your next step. Learn to use your own body, the machine, by knowing its parts and when they feel like they are working as well as when they need tuning up.

So when is it your heart speaking and when is it your ego? What is the craving for food really telling you? Do you know when you need something and what that thing is? Do you know how to control yourself? What is that headache telling you? Why do you keep reliving the same relationship patterns? Do you know what to do to nurture yourself, heal yourself, and get back in the driver's seat of your life?

Via mindfulness and learning to know yourself, you become a clear, concentrated, full embodiment of your unique essence. You become the conscious creator of your days, the magician of your life.

3

you are an energy
perceived as a body

E nergy. It's real. Energy is everywhere. The
sun's light is energy; the plants that use it are
energy. When you eat the plants, you eat all
the energy contained in the plant, which is the energy
of the sun mixed with the energy of the water, the air,
and the minerals in the soil. Everything you perceive
is energy—arranged in varied ways with different
levels of density and consciousness. You are a unique
configuration of energy. You change and grow in
accordance with what you experience and absorb.

People describe *feeling* energetic or say they are
lacking energy as a way to describe their level of
vibrancy, which we can envision as a lamp glowing
brightly or dimly. When they feel low or dim, they
reach for things to boost them—like caffeine or a nap.
Inherently, they know they are made of energy. In the
same way that sound has vibration, frequency, and

volume, you do, too. It's perceptible and measurable. You are an energetic being, from the tiniest component of your DNA to the comprehensive collective referred to as humanity.

Energy shifts and changes. You, as energy, shift and change. Your emotions are energy, energy in motion. Your words are energy—just like sound emitted from an instrument. Your thoughts are energy, too. Energy does not disappear. It only transmutates. As established in the previous chapters, you are the magician of your energy. You decide what the energy feels like, what to do with it, and how to influence it.

Notice how things outside of you change your energy. How does food affect you? How about sound, music, silence? Does your body respond to the cycles of the moon, astrological events, the weather, seasonal shifts? Do places like the beach, the mountains, a city, a museum, or a graveyard affect you? Does the structure of a room or a daily schedule affect your energy? Can you be shifted by what is around you?

On the flip side, can you also create impact with your own energy? Yes! This is a major part of being a conscious creator. It is an important part of taking control and living well in body, mind, and soul.

Check in on your energy. Begin to notice what you're feeling and what the influences upon it are. Use mindfulness and yoga, exercise and breath work, meditation and creative expression to keep your energy in a high vibration, leaving you feeling better, lighter, more positive. This can be as simple as closing your eyes, feeling where your feet are connected to the Earth, and noticing the breath entering and exiting your nose.

Carefully choosing what you allow into your energetic field is important. Everything is energy and affects other energy. There is polarization and a constant dance between the kinds of energy that we can access and emit. Through carefully honing your own authority over your own energy and coming to intimately know yourself, you can know what promotes your best vibe. Carefully choose what you say, do, watch, and eat; how you move; whose words you consume; and where you go.

Notice the flow of energy between you and the world around you. How does lighting make you feel at different times—sunrise, cloudy days, dim rooms, fluorescent lights? What do different types of food do to you? Go through the huge world and really get a sense of your interaction with the whole thing.

Figure out a recipe—a shifting, modifiable one—that can change often to provide what is best for you in all situations. Preside over your energy as the master of you that you are.

Through experimenting, come to know what raises you to a higher, more fulfilling energetic frequency. Rather than jumping out of bed and rushing through a mindless list of to-do's, which could shift your energy into the doldrums of boredom, lack, and generally low energy, experiment with waking up a little earlier to give yourself time and space to mindfully arrange your energy.

Play with the best way to wake up. What alarm sound is most effective at waking you in a happy mood? Does hitting snooze make you feel happier or more sluggish? What are the first things your eyes fall upon when you rise: something beautiful and inspiring or a pile of dirty laundry? How does this impact you? When you move into your bathroom, what does it feel like in there—a place of beauty and nurturing or cluttered? When you begin preparing yourself for the day, is there a sense of care or just a sequence of improvements being acted out? How does the lighting feel and is there anything you see that sparks a feeling of love, joy, or inspiration?

For example, inside my vanity cabinet door, I have a few stickers and quotes that help me remember who I am at my highest. Gazing at them as I brush my teeth instantly transports me to a higher, more uplifted, positive frequency. I recall how I felt when I was traveling and bought that sticker or I relate once again to the name and description of the goddess energy described on the quarter page article I have taped there.

It is important to partake in a regular cleansing of your energy. In the same way you would shower away the dirt on your body, take time to cleanse your energy. How will you know what a cleansing routine looks like for you? Tune in and check in. Try various practices to notice what feels best.

A simple practice to begin your day feeling well is to wake up and care for yourself in a nurturing way. Breathe in fresh new air, fill with new life force energy (called *prana*). Nourish your skin and hair with oils, your muscles with stretching, your belly with good nutrients. Uplift yourself for the day ahead by listening to positive, inspiring lectures, prayers, or music. Morning meditation is the most amazing way to begin the day centered, whole, and clear.

Experiment with additional self-care rituals in the morning such as dry-brushing your skin, consciously absorbing the blessing of warm clean water in the shower, and oiling the body or massaging lotion into your skin. While you care for yourself, allow positive loving thoughts to permeate your body, raising your energy through loving care.

Make time to sit and pray or meditate for a few minutes before you interact with any outside energy. This allows you to be clear and self-directed, at the wheel of your own ship energetically, before you are touched by outside energies.

As you go about your day, be cautious as to which external stories you are allowing into your day. Ask if they are adding to your resonance of beauty and abundance or depleting and stress-inducing.

Similarly, remember to cleanse your energy after leaving your workplace or being in a stressful situation. This is simple to do. Just use the power of your creative mind to envision yourself energetically showering away any lingering energy, anxiety, resentment, hostility, or other strings connecting you to those stressful events or people. Let them slide off and away as a shower of pure positive energy rains down on you. These mindful practices take self-care and energy maintenance to a deeper level just by using the power of an intentionally focused mind.

At the end of a day, begin to collect yourself and reflect after a day of interacting with outside energies. Burn off extra energy with a strong walk or exercise practice, feed your body nourishing food and prepare to calm the nervous system with a warm shower or bath, journaling, and getting cozy.

Be sure to enact simple yet powerful practices to help you close out your day, such as walking, jogging, practicing yoga, journaling, or resting in nature. At the end of your day, imagine coming home to your beautiful haven and leaving anything heavy on the doorstep so you can begin self-restoration practices. Recall for yourself, without judgment, the things that shifted your energy, then utilize the best practices to bring your energy back to a comfortable "end of the day" level. This will likely be a different set of practices than the ones employed to start your day. Bringing yourself back to calm and ready to enjoy the evening is important for establishing healthy circadian rhythms. Ending the day with gratitude and a practice of reflection is a nice way to clear away the lingering energies that might affect your sleep or your relationships.

Energy maintenance is a practice of really paying attention and then following through to make the necessary changes. You must have courage and discipline to do what is truly best for you. Often, that means choosing to eat a certain way, to exercise when it's easier to skip it, to rest when you need to, and to cut out anything and anyone who adds negativity to your energy or causes you to turn against your own best interests. Fear is always lurking, trying to get inside through our weak spots and lower energy moments. It is important to be immersed in self-knowing and self-care at all times.

Conversely, be cognizant of the energy you are putting out to other people, the energy you bring to a group or situation outwardly and even in a subtle psychic way. Remember, there is a constant exchange of energy. As a master magician, you can create a world that you most desire, one that supports the well-being of all involved, simply by being aware of your most subtle energies. Notice when a word shifts you. Tune in to how others respond when they receive a smile from you. Take note of a text message's tone. Energy exchange is both subtle and the most powerful form of communication and action you can take.

You are an energetic, magnetic being. As you start to notice what you are drawn to and what comes toward you, you will gain information about your point of attraction. Always check in with what is flowing in and out.

A powerful practice is to note when you are stuck in whirlpools of behavior that bring your energy down. Sometimes a behavior or relationship that initially gave you a feeling of being uplifted will, with time or repetition, bring you down, ultimately dimming your energy. For instance, one day you might stop for a happy hour drink after work, connect with nice friends, and feel joy. The remembrance of this uplifting feeling might cause you to repeat this behavior the next day and the next. Even if you don't get the same resulting feeling of being uplifted, you might repeat this for weeks on end, waiting to feel that initial exhilaration of connection, fun, and uplifting only to realize that it had developed into a pattern that is not good for you. If you don't stop to actually ask yourself about the energetics going on, you can begin a pattern of self-sabotage. The energy you were seeking had the resonance of connection, fun, and upliftment. The energy you stayed in did not. In the end, you were left with a lower vibration.

As energetic, magnetic beings, we are constantly delivering and receiving energy. Become a master of your energetic resonance. This is the power you have for holding a strong, clear beacon of your own poetic essence. This is how you positively, actively create the world around you.

4
rainbows and fairies

Okay, don't roll your eyes at that chapter title yet. Please just see where this goes. In addition to being an energetic being, you are also a multidimensional being. Dimension is the degree to which we perceive things. The words you are reading right now are two-dimensional, a contrast of one thing to another. The item you are reading the words from—a paper, computer screen, or book—is three-dimensional. It has height, width, and depth. You are reading this in your four-dimensional life that has height, weight, and depth plus one more component: time. It takes time for your eyes to read the words and for the words and ideas to be processed.

But what about the concepts we are discussing? Where does something like love fit into the world we have measured and quantified so neatly? Love isn't any of the above, so what is it? It is multidimensional.

It is beyond space, beyond time, beyond measurement. However, it is still perceptible.

Do you just shrug and allow it to be what it is without questioning its existence? After all, you have felt the energy of love in many of its forms via your receptors. You have openly accepted your ability to feel love, to experience it, to bask in it. You agree it exists. You agree that although you cannot see, hear, or sense love through your five senses, it exists because in some other way we are perceiving it. There are more ways to sense. There are more ways of being. There is more out there.

Discovering the next level of dimensionality requires you to accept the existence of a thing despite being unable to quantify it or perceive it with your five senses. Here is an example: Although science has not officially endorsed that we have an energetic chakra system consisting of light, colors, and measurable vibratory energies, it is easy to accept, through logic and reasoning, that energy chakras exist. Chakras make sense when we learn about them—especially when you learn how to use your own dormant abilities to feel the energy moving in them and how their energetic frequencies are related to your state of being. However, people often need to learn how to reignite this dormant skill of perception because, as humans, we are taught to know our world through the five senses. You weren't made aware of your ability to perceive energy in a way outside of the five senses.

Being confined to the beliefs and dynamics of a four-dimensional world view is limiting. Our social constructs have molded us to believe in the things science has proven and have trained us, through constructed narratives, to disbelieve in the more esoteric.

You were taught that there is a limit to your world, with confines to live safely within it. The widely accepted world system of interaction thrives on this limited perception. It serves to keep people living small, accepting only that which can be sensed through five senses, which is a much easier world for the system to control than a limitless one. There is great potential when people fully function as divine multi-dimensional beings. Whereas the system is able to manipulate reality when everyone is agreeing to the same limited version of reality, imagine the power a collective humanity has once they awaken to their full potential as multidimensional, magical creators!

So who is to say what is real and what isn't if reality is based in perception? How can anything be negated or affirmed? If you perceive or imagine something, it is created on some level. It might be a blurry, far-off version that isn't quite saturated enough in another person's reality for them to perceive it, but it does exist on some level in some dimension. Just because I am unable to perceive something you perceive does not make it unreal. So then, aren't there endless exis-tences? There are as many as we can all create with the spontaneous and instantaneous spark of our minds. There is absolute power in communing to share our magic and our visions. As powerful creators, uniting our energies is the way to create a dimension of heaven on Earth. Together we can create beautiful stories and actually live their reality.

In the limited perception world, we were influenced to believe that things like fairies are figures of the imagination, angels are a possibility, aliens are for freaks to believe in, and evil forces are part of Hollywood thrillers. The wide acceptance that these all actually exist gets a chuckle and sometimes a scoff. Who is to say these don't exist, though, when so many people have stories that suggest they might? Why can't these exist in dimensionality that most people just haven't been taught how to perceive yet? Why are some people psychic and others not so much? What if the ability to know, to create, to live very differently is just on the other side of belief and being open to it?

Perhaps, as humans evolve as a species and allow one another to hold their own truths, the shared reality will be more expansive and magical, too. Perhaps opening to our multidimensional selves is key to the evolution of the human species. What if seeing a rainbow isn't just a visual experience, but actually a gateway to another paradigm? What if there are codes in the colors that remind humans of their true essence as beings of light? As you allow yourself to believe in and hold your own perceptions, also allow all other perceptions and imaginations to be actualized possibilities, too. And with your conscious focus upon any of them, you can assist in further focusing them into a shared reality.

These open possibilities are, perhaps, similar to the visions used in technological advancements. Whereas early man focused creativity on developing tools he made with his hands over a fire or with a knife, today's humans are creating virtual space and expanding our perception of reality in cyberspace. Creativity is key. Magical thinking is key. Being open to things beyond the current perception is where innovation occurs. This is the point where you get to acknowledge that your magic matters, your sensitivity matters. Accessing the ancient wisdom, the innate technology that has gone dormant inside of yourself is key to evolving.

Accepting that you are multidimensional will allow you to find deeper levels of truth and help you access important information for your survival and ability to thrive. By opening to beings and information that exist in other dimensions beyond what is accepted as our limited reality, you might find powerful ways to heal yourself and the planet—even the universe. Expanding perception might guide you to ultimate love, complete wholeness.

We are multidimensional beings with a general lack of understanding regarding our vastness, our capacity, our skills, and our power to expand and be. If we surpass our limited concept of life, the universe, time, space, and our five senses, our entire way of life can morph into the next expression of human life. It is with this imagination that we create new realities. The word "imagining" to me is "I am a genie–ing," as in, "I am making my magic come true." See, everything begins with an idea, nurtured with desire and energy before it becomes manifest. So using our multidimensionality is not outlandish; it is essential. Our natural desire to imagine, to create, to expand is part of the beauty of our being-ness. We are human BEings, mastering the art of BEing, which would mean that it is our nature to imagine first and then step into the BEingness of that imagined vision, thought, feeling.

Many people report traveling to different realms, time-traveling to alternate lives, or experiencing love in a completely massive and all-encompassing way via meditation. Meditation is a tool you can use to place the logical mind and sensory perceptions in the off position and awaken your usually dormant modes of perception.

This is what enlightenment feels like. It is pure consciousness channeled through a sense we don't yet have a name for and feels like bliss and love moving through your entire being, but even your being feels like the oneness of the whole universe inside and around you, so massive, alive, and radiant. This is way more than one can perceive through the five senses. The dimensionality is much higher vibrationally than our human body, so it requires that you prepare to match the resonance by clearing away lower vibrational energies that are within your field. Becoming more of your pure divine self helps you be able to hold higher energies for longer periods of time.

People who can consistently do this have been few and far between. Often, yogis and Buddhist monks who spend their days away from low-vibrational influences and instead stay in high vibration were more conducive containers for receiving higher dimensional wisdom and energy. Getting beyond, to the openness to more expansive energy is what brings us closer to consistent contentment.

Meditation is the very best way to create space inside of ourselves for all of the best things to occur. The space we create while we meditate heals us, guides us, and animates the divine spirit inside. This point of attraction aligns us effortlessly with the highest timelines and greatest flow. Meditation allows us to go from the hardened path of "reality" to a spacious dimension of love-filled expansion. In this expansiveness, you grow, change, and rearrange your energy signature to one that is more aligned with what most people desire: abundance. One comes out of meditation restored and whole. A connection is formed with what could be.

It is interesting to note the widespread acceptance of how transformational it can be to go to a spa, salon, or counseling session, yet how much society underestimates the results of sitting in silence and going deeply into oneself. However, there is a growing understanding that the gateway to metamorphosis starts by going inside of our own holy temple. It is the gateway to accessing our multidimensional selves and claiming our oneness with all that is, even the fairies and unicorns.

5
your body is a physical masterpiece

I n the same way that we can feel good vibes and low vibes, we have opportunities to influence our bodies on a cellular level daily with our input and output of energy. You can add and subtract from your physical body in ways that achieve the highest and most harmonious vibrations, allowing you to feel your best and to be the most powerful generator. In this way, you create a body that stays supple and strong, healthy and vibrant.

When you choose to ingest foods and beverages that exist at low vibrational levels, such as sugary and fatty foods, and take in depressive chemicals like alcohol, you lower your body's vibration. The body needs to shift down, like a manual car transmission, to process the food and use a junkier level of fuel. Sometimes you interpret this downshift as feeling better, like when you drink a glass of wine or eat your favorite comfort food. The slowing down and lowering of energy can almost feel like comfort when you have been operating in a consistent state of anxiety. In those instances, you are simply blanketing nervousness and chaotic energy with lower vibes.

Sometimes you choose the opposite: caffeine and chemicals that amp you up to a faster, seemingly higher vibration. These are short-term crutches. Afterward, you end up crashing down lower than where you began.

The key is to keep yourself consistently functioning at a high vibration is through a steady stream of healthy and high-vibrational foods that do not encourage short-term fixes nor try to solve matters of the heart and mind with a quick fix. Food for the body should be looked at as fuel for the cells. Remedies for healing and balancing your mental and emotional health can also be found in food, but only foods based on the inherent wisdom of nature's plan. Herbs and foods are meant to be used in a wise way to balance our systems. All we need for perfect health exists in nature. The closer you eat to the source of sunlight, the more radiant your health will be. Plant-based eating is the best, foods untouched by chemicals and in season to extract the purest energy.

Eating meat is a personal choice but deserves to be looked at in the energetic exchange that occurs in the life and death of the animal in comparison to the human. If the animal has lived well and eaten cleanly, not been injected with hormones and chemicals to make it grow better or be more resistant to illness, and been peacefully and respectfully allowed to live and die well, it might be good for your body in terms of giving you what you need. For many, the process of eating animals and animal by-products like dairy and eggs provides a much lower vibration of nutrition than a plant-based diet. The elements used to bring animals to our plates in modern society are so fouled that their vibration is quite low. Eating low-vibe food will decrease a person's vibration. There is not, however, a mandated measurement of vibration. Eating is a chemical and energetic experience, and only you can decide what is best for your overall highest expression.

Detoxifying your body is equally important. Knowing how to cleanse the body and nourish it are incredibly important to keeping your machine working well and vibrating high. The body needs to be cleansed of the elements that aren't supportive of high vibrations. It is essential to regularly exercise, exchanging the old energies and toxins for refreshing new energies, or prana, through breathing in the new and out the old, sweating, and chemically though the contraction and expansion of the muscles and connective tissue.

Occasional fasting to encourage the body to switch from its normal patterning and eliminate the junk it might have stored is a valuable practice. I suggest speaking to an expert about fasting and detoxifying to learn what is best for your specific body. You can benefit from massage and yoga, tai chi, and stretching to loosen connective tissue and release the emotions and toxins stored therein. Drinking plenty of clean spring water daily flushes out and eliminates anything not serving us on a cellular level, too.

Our diet is not only what you eat and drink, but also what you allow yourself to absorb from the outside world. The words, music, news, and visual stimuli we take in affect our energy and therefore our bodies. Being in a constant stream of intake and output is paramount in the human experience and is the bedrock of what life is all about, but you must be cautious of how your external environment and stimuli affect your emotions and mental well-being. In addition to digesting food and beverages, the external stimuli you intake affect the biochemical arrangement of your energy, which presents itself in the form of BEing. All of these affect the degree of your well-being, which determines your state of good health or illness and disease.

The key teaching is always "know thyself," and in the process of getting to know yourself, you must be a witness to the flow into and out of you. Notice keenly the effect that all that you interact has upon you. Begin to tune into how you feel in each moment of your day, noticing the varying effects of the people, places, and things you move in and among and how they make you feel. Notice your own choices and your own output, as well.

The way you feed off the grid of life is all affecting your BEing, including your physical body. This is why it is so important to disconnect from the busyness of your world and spend time in nature. It is essential to even momentarily take breaks to create pauses in your intake of external chatter and stimuli. Even small periods of rest and breaks for mindfulness, visualization, breath work, and movement are beneficial to take measure and keep you anchored in your sovereignty when things around you begin to affect your energetic and physical body.

Your thoughts and memory also direct the energy of, and therefore the health of, your body. For instance, a visual stimulus is actually a neutral charge. Whether it triggers you positively or negatively is determined by what your mind, data, and memory, bring to the event. For example, seeing a clown can fill you with joy or spark terror based on previous memories of how you have interacted with the concept of clown in the past. Likewise, eating a green bean can be a delicious experience of dining on nature's bounty or it can feel like a punishment because a parent demanded you eat your veggies.

This is where diving deep into your past traumas helps. You can rewrite the programs that automatically direct our minds and therefore our bodies. You can go into your history and heal the traumas that continue to direct your present experiences. So many of us are walking around in bodies that are carrying stories from ages ago. These stories are faulty or even untrue, collected in times of trauma and often at such a young and impressionable age that they go undetected as subconscious patterns. By having the courage to dive in and see the thoughts, experience the memories, and correct the untruths, you can heal your body and mind. You will peel off layers that are hiding your true nature of perfect health and abundant wellness.

By choosing the way you work with your body energetically, you can begin the process of living in higher vibration, resonating with purity, abundance, freedom, and joy. Feed your body, your vehicle, well to vibe high.

6
you are connected to all that is

In chapter one, we discussed your constant manifestation of the outside world based on your relationship to it, and we can then assume that nothing that is meant for you will ever miss you. In the constant exchange between you and the reality you perceive around you, there are no mistakes. Even the things that seem like they went wrong or things you believe you lost are just being filtered through the limited human perspective of a seemingly linear life that you try to make comprehensible. Everything, whether you perceive it as good or bad, is perfect in the eyes of the divine. "All that is" means all of it. And you, as a created element of divine will, are a part of that.

Before you came to this world, you received a mission. You agreed to experience certain things for the education and experience of your soul. You decided these major and minor lessons while you were in spirit form, where there is only unconditional love and a deep desire to feel contrast in order to experience your soul's great capacity for variation and expansion. You choose the twists and turns and encounters you will have before you are an embodied human, and therefore without the fears and aversions of the ego's perspective.

You were okay with the twists and turns and the humanness of your experience before you even incarnate, in fact, you wanted it. There is a desire to experience it. It is your greatest joy and your purpose in the grand plan of life to enter this dimension and experience duality and the vastness of creative potential, knowing that you are about to experience something that is not your actual nature, something that does not define you.

Once you get here, to this body, this plane of existence, your understanding changes a bit. The veil of the program takes over, and you see life from an obscured vantage point. The human world is run on a program that is constantly being added to by the collective of humans. In this program, duality reigns supreme. There is always polarity between opposites here: good/bad, light/dark, happy/sad, rich/poor, healthy/sick, victim/aggressor. Within this duality, you are constantly trying to find yourself. Humans strive to know our true nature within these polarities. It is easy to believe you are separate from everything else because you see it outside of yourself, in your field of perception.

On the Earth plane, rules are built into the program that cause people to strive to be worthy enough, smart enough, and strong enough to survive. The rules of the program implore that doing enough keeps us alive and united with others, that we must earn our share of energy from the externals. Worthiness, as we perceive it within the program, keeps us alive. Chasing worthiness, which becomes the goal, keeps people from remembering their innermost truth, the truth that you are connected to all that is, that you are whole and therefore holy, that you are everything and connected to all there is.

Until one awakens to the truth of their connectedness, life can feel Pin the Tail on the Donkey. During this initial period, you are constantly deciding where the tail should go on the donkey, blindfolded, spun around a few times, and aiming somewhere in an unseen space. Often we discover that we made a mistake, weren't accurate, so we self-judge and create even more separation from ourselves and the perfection of our divinity. In doing this, we affirm that we are not good enough, not divine, and we recommit to the program that got us to this point in the first place. We are saying, *"Nope, that didn't make me feel better, I need to strive more."*

Eventually, we realize that removing the blindfold and being able to see clearly eliminates the entire game.

The blindfold of the human world, the program that we are in, is the concept that keeps us from actually seeing and being the divine manifestor of our own amazing creation. It keeps us ignorant to the fact that we are connected to all that is and that by removing our blindfold, we will clearly see how to connect to all that is. After discarding the blindfold, we see that our mistakes are just part of our initial plan to play here in our humanness.

The bigger truth of the pin-the-tail experience is that you are here to learn more about being a human, to gain and accumulate experiences that direct you to the clear seeing and knowing of your divine essence. We are not here to get it "right" by human measurements, not here to earn it from worthiness, not here to pin it on and be perfect. We already are perfect embodiments of God. We are on this journey to realize our connection to all that is, to our source, to our innate ability to manifest and live our highest, best lives of exploring this world and our way in it.

Knowing that you cannot get it wrong because it is all right, and that there are many avenues for you to gain experience, all with congratulations waiting at the end, allows you to rest, knowing that there is nothing that will miss you. You will always attract and choose the best match for you at any given time, in any space.

This means you don't need to regret nor go backward to wishing it were different. Just live in each moment, learn from the past, and make new choices moving forward. By using the result of each aligned or contrasted experience, we get the chance to make a new desire on our next step. Connecting all these steps is the way we keep walking through life.

When we remain rooted in past experience with regret and focus on the contrasts of what we wanted versus what we got, we stay stuck in victim mode, regretting and wishing for a different outcome. We can become depressed. Forgetting our ultimate plan, our innate perfection, can lead us down a path of low vibrational thoughts and beliefs. However, constantly remembering that our contrasts are here by design and do not define us, but rather, help direct us, is the magic solution. While we think the experience is happening *to* us, it is actually happening *for* and *with* us.

When we lean too far into the future and worry that we will miss or mistake something, we become anxious. Knowing and embodying the concept that we are connected to all that is, to the magician energy, and combining that with the knowing that anything meant for us will not miss us because of the law of attraction and that there are no mistakes allows us to live in freedom. It lets us relax, breathe, and lessen our tight hold on what we perceive as reality and right and wrong.

Remembering that this world is a playing field for us to explore helps us live in the constructs of time and space more easily, too. We relax into knowing that all is aligning in divine timing and that we are always exactly where we need to be at exactly the time we are supposed to be there because there are truly no supposed to's. "Should" is a bad word, generally pointing us to dig into our belief system and the inner chatter we are aligning with. That inner chatter is seldom the voice of God, and it's seldom from the loving divinity within. Relax and know that the magic within you has unlimited resources and power. Go to your heart and know your true essence. Be guided by inspiration.

If you know that what's meant for you is easily achievable, then you begin to release your resistance to those goals. You neutralize the opposing laws of attraction and relax into the flow of knowing that what is yours will always come to you. Relaxing into the flow of your own divine life experience can be a joyous journey of being ever present and feeling good consistently as the tensions and pressures fall away.

Not worrying about past mistakes and releasing limited beliefs launches you forward onto a path of creating a life of ever-unfolding experience. From that solid inner core of knowing your divine truth of existence, your forward movement feels aligned with all that is and becomes independent of the programming confinements you might have worked within your whole life.

7

the magnificent power of the heart

The heart is not secondary to the brain and the mind. The heart is the leading edge. In modern society, the head has been valued for its innovation and logic, for industrial and scientific advancements we have celebrated as they seemingly made our lives better, longer, and easier. In the modern view, the heart is seen as soft in a way that seems weak. However, the heart is our largest emanation of energy and our most major chakra of integration between the heavenly above and the Earthly below. It is the main creation point for being a human.

The power of the human heart—not just the blood pumping organ, but the energetic heart—is the reason for and the creation of why we are us, why we act, why we live. The heart is the avenue for all that is. What we feel sticks, and therefore creates.

The heart is the avenue for experiencing emotional pleasure and pain, and these then create pathways in the mind. The stronger the feeling from the heart, the more we learn. It's our beacon. The greatest way to teach is to appeal to a student's heart, to his or her deep humanness. This is how we make the best connections with others and feel expansion in our souls.

The heart is our main mode of communication. We communicate more with our hearts than with our minds and mouths. We can feel that another has love for us before they even speak a word. We can heal a roomful of people by going into our heart and radiating out the love of source. We listen to powerful speakers, and we are moved. We respond not because of the words, but because of hearts.

Via our hearts, we are easily influenced, inspired, or repulsed. For good or for evil, this power has moved many throughout history. Consider how Hitler's dark heart impressed others enough to become murderers. Consider Jesus and how his heart taught others how to love and heal. We can create a spark of enlightenment with our very presence, and this comes from our hearts.

It is also via our hearts that we can enter into the deepest recesses of our being. We can access our information across years, lifetimes, and dimensions via the portal of our living hearts. In this radiant place, we connect with and have communion with all that is.

When we willingly accept the vulnerability of our humanness, we go into the heart to reconcile our experiences, and if we go deep enough inside, we meet our divinity, which tells us it is okay, it is all right. Our hearts hold inside of them the doorway to complete peace and acceptance of every experience, understanding each morsel in ways the mind cannot ever grasp. The heart is the connection to a higher form of knowing, beyond our human capacity within the duality of our worldly experience.

Through the heart, we channel healing for our entire being, affecting the energy of our DNA and rewriting our own programs. Our heart is the doorway to all that is. We feel here our traumas as they connect to our fears and concerns. This is the place of healing them once they are felt. The heart is the container for our growth, for finding our wholeness. Your heart is pure. It is only the misconstrued data that plays with your mind and alters your perfect understanding of what you perceive as reality.

It follows then that important missions on Earth are to go deeply into our heart space, to heal wounds, to witness experiences without getting stuck in them, and then to do the work of purifying our heart, enabling this magnetic powerhouse to work in pure, divine form as the force of goodness.

8
the pole shift to oneness

The energetic nature we have touched upon so far is the very basis of how we live and how our reality is constructed. It is the bonding of atoms, the deciding factor in how configuration occurs. It is a determination of, or measure of, strength, capacity, and endurance, and it is all based on magnetics. This relates us back to the law of attraction. Like attracts like. This also means lack attracts lack. If our system is screaming out "I cannot accumulate wealth," or "I cannot lose weight," then our reality is reflecting back that same lack. As long as that is the dial to which you have set your resonance, either knowingly or unknowingly, you will attract that exact reality right back to you.

Quick story: I was stuck rather unknowingly in a resonance of victim. Having a troubled childhood relationship with my parents from an early age, I attracted a husband who reiterated that resonance, mistreating me yet again. I got into dependency mode, codependency mode, in fact, which kept me from standing on my own two feet. I kept living out the same pattern over and over: try hard to be good, get abandoned. I could not make things manifest as well as I had wished because I was at a deep level in the vibe of not being worthy of it. My underlying story to the universe, which I was subtly whispering over and over, was "I will give and give, and you can take and take." Once I healed this, I felt completely different— like someone hit a reset button. I had been attracting a pattern of utter lack. My lack attracted more patterns of lack. The undercurrent of who I was, despite my actions, integrity, and intentions to always be aligned with goodness, carried the resonance of being wounded, codependent, mistreated, and lacking.

One day as I sat in meditation, I was praying to the absolute most high, and while I pictured my concept of what this is, which was a radiant sea of pearlescent light, I was naming it "mother father God, Christ, God, Highest Love of all Loves." As I did, I saw instantly that we are all attempting to achieve oneness —yoga, union, unity—which really means aligning our concept of duality: masculine and feminine, give and take, negative and positive, light and shadow, these polarized energies, into homeostasis, into balance like nature: ONENESS. The God I was sensing was that exact oneness.

Oneness means eliminating the gap between, creating a merge, uniting one out of duality. The one true God is not many. It is composed of many, but it is one because it is in ultimate balance and unity and has ascended past the layers of duality and polarity of energy. It is all in ONE.

I had never understood God to be this before. I have learned the components of God, have become intimate in my own healing of my own mother and father wounds with the energy of divine masculine love and divine feminine love, but I had not understood the bliss of complete union. It is what I had been seeking in my life forever: the energy of the union I wished to have with another. However, I have known this oneness deep down forever. I came wired for it, knowing it is my ultimate mission. I thought it was with another person, my life partner, and while I do still want to experience that, I could now see the truth of our energy and the whole point of the game: We come here to ascend past duality. We come to find our union inside of ourselves. That is the path of knowing, of finding bliss. God is the goal. Union is the mission. While we live in a perceived duality, we must find unity.

This mission to attain bliss and union, to find God, to shift the poles from *dual to oneness* is the reason yogis went off alone into the wilderness to seek. It is what Jesus lived and taught as the path back to God. Once we understand that a union with God means a union with our own parts, a healing and purifying of what we have accumulated from all the years of interacting with a world that gives us a fragmented sense of things, it allows us to do the work. As we heal and grow, we can begin to play as humans in the Earth plane. As healed, blissful people, the law of attraction pulls together like individuals, divine partners, and that level of both actualization and divine partnership on Earth will be massively explosive. When we get to this level of existence as humans, we clear the world of its pain and duality. In our romanticized world, we are so obsessed with seeking love in another. We weren't told the whole story. Yes, we are to seek the kingdom of God first—because then all else is added. Of course, this is true. If we do, we set our resonance to heaven on Earth, and then the world shifts, and we live better, higher, freer.

Sadly, seeking God has been intentionally disfigured. Many religious sects have made the seeking of God into a punishing path and kept the image of God as something outside of us. God is depicted as the man on the throne in the sky who is a harsh judge. While this might be based loosely in the same dualistic, polarity-based philosophy of good vs. evil, light vs. dark, we need to remember that the work is inside of ourselves. The duality feels real, and the mission is to see beyond the veil of illusion to the truth of God that all is one. This is what I received during mediation that day. Oneness is the goal. Polarity is the sin, the swamp we tread on our way back to wholeness.

Our job is truly to seek all that keeps the gap open and heal those beliefs and wounds so that the divide can heal, so it becomes once again whole, one, unified. This is an energetic attraction. The opposites have to become so neutralized that there is an ability for the poles to come into balance, to align instead of repel. The force is love, and the closer we come to *being love*, the more we allow the poles to merge. We shift from fragmented to whole.

There truly is one God, one whole perfection from which all the parts originate. We begin there, we return there. It is our job here on Earth to shift the planetary resonance to come into wholeness on our own, by healing the wounds inside of us, by bringing ourselves into the most complete and balanced, most in-love energy we possibly can, by being God. We are God, in formation.

When we actualize this, we radiate a light of our own, a sort of sun, or halo, an aura of light, and the radiance of full love, full alignment, full creative capacity. We become a true beacon of light, of loving presence. This is what followers of Christ felt, what followers of Buddha felt. This is the loving presence, not derived from egoic service to others in martyrdom as we are taught from church and society, but from the only true energetic alignment, which is the love derived from deep and true healing, merging of the divine feminine and divine masculine energies. It comes from oneness inside, which is the light that is shone from inner union.

We see glimpses of this when we are in love with another. We shine, we float, we are blissful because we have a taste of what union is like. This is not the end game of course, but a taste of it. It's a carrot to keep us in motion, to keep our stubborn selves moving toward healing.

In these romantic relationships, we are motivated to move toward healing in ways that being solo would possibly not motivate. It is the moving of the particles, the little charged atoms, informing us of where we still need to heal ourselves. Relationships provide information for how to get closer to our God-self—how to achieve union within. They point us to the old wounds, the little inner children who are still waiting for the love, the outstretched hand of adult you, wiser you, safer you, to bring them back, to bridge the space of their hurt spots, their wounds. Soothing them soothes all. It brings our fragmented parts back into wholeness. The triggering from our loved ones is often a signal to examine what is not whole, where there is a lack of love. Where is healing still needed?

I pray all people will heal and become whole. Yoga, energy work, having healers around me as well as my team of angels and guides, have helped me to heal and realize my divinity. My work is not done, of course. There are always ways to get closer to God. I have much to do to find full union. But I am grateful for this leg of the journey. There are so many tools and pathways to resolve our polarity into united divinity. Finding yours, exploring multiple tools, will result in healing, wholeness. Union is worth it.

The reflection provided by our loved ones, especially in times of conflict or pressure, allows us to ask, "Where is healing still needed?"

9
restorative union

The restoration of love, peace, and harmony to Mother Earth will happen via the restoration of divine union.

Since I was a little girl, I have known in my heart that I came here to find my counterpart, my sacred groom, so that we would unite our powers, in complementary style, and live well. This is the way to bring Heaven to Earth. This is how we change things; this is how we raise the consciousness of the planet in the most powerful of ways: through bringing two healed people in love together in flesh and in spirit. There is nothing more powerful than love. There is a reason it is called "making love." What I didn't know as a little girl was that I would first need to find my own inner love. I would need to take a wild journey, experiencing much of what is not whole, much of what resides in the polarities and shadows of lack, in order to come into love. I would need to understand it all in order to find my balance within and until then, I had a lot of healing to do.

The balance of inner feminine and masculine is a polarity thing, as mentioned previously. We must balance inside of us the aspects of masculine energy, which are action, doing, logic, steady endurance like the sun, with aspects of feminine energy, which are receptive, creative, feeling, intuition, nurturing, cyclical like the moon. We feel attracted to another because we are each polarized one way or the other: masculine or feminine. This is the tricky part. In divine form, this is the highest ideal, to be charged as one or the other is magnetic and pure, but it requires a person who has faced their shadows, healed themselves, found their own balance, healing, and their own inner connection to God, in order for one to be divinely masculine or divinely feminine.

Most often, we are polarized but not divinely so, because of negative programming from society and wounds. The wounded feminine feels the shadow sides of receptive energy: passivity, overly giving, poor boundaries, and unworthiness. She might feel resentful toward the masculine or take on masculine expression because she is in self-protection mode.

The wounded masculine, in its negative shadow aspect, comes across as overly polarized as demanding, controlling, greedy, disconnected from emotions, defined by achievements or lack thereof. He might grasp onto his inner feminine aspects of emotions with shame and can come across as resentful toward the feminine, untrusting and unwilling to give himself to her.

This is the connection we have witnessed between masculine and feminine for centuries. It forms unhealthy unions and our ability to connect in partnership and feel fulfilled has failed drastically.

This is due to two people coming together, very much in states of disillusionment about themselves, needing their own healing. Society has set people up, over the past 2,000 or so years, during the age of Pisces, to believe in a patriarchal worshipping. We have been taught that God is male, the feminine is only valuable for birthing, and that union of male and female is not the beautiful, sacred enriching experience of ecstatic long-lasting fulfillment that it is. Too many stories have been told to separate our masculine and feminine from one another, to create distrust and devalue union. The story of betrayal and abuse has been retold and reproduced over and over, and we as a society have lost our ability to trust in what we know deep down we desire.

However, countless stories have also been told throughout time expressing the power of love, the adventure of two lovers finding one another, and how that ignites a passion for life and thriving. From

Cinderella to *I Love Lucy*, the story goes that a good man and a good woman achieve much happiness from their union. We can see how the balance within the relationship, the shared oneness of each half's strengths, creates an empowered whole.

In more recent decades, many attempts have been made in society to break down the concept of union, with examples of soap opera affairs, reality TV shows choosing partners as a game, and movie star relationships that highlight the brevity and complexity of the new form of marriage. The family unit has taken a major hit with the dissolution of a mindful, sacred union at the core of marriage. The examples we see of a healthy dynamic are rare.

The truth of the matter is that the divine masculine and the divine feminine are a force to be reckoned with as they meet and join together. The polarity of male and female, the plus and the minus, the magnetics of the union, are powerful enough to create miracles—to create new life, but also to manifest dreams, wishes, and shifts in paradigms. The power of the divine masculine and divine feminine coming together is the Holy Grail. It is the chalice, the vessel that holds magical elixir.

What the divine intended for us was for the masculine energy to hold the feminine with such conviction, such steadfastness, such protective adoration that she can then feel safe to unfurl and expand, like the petals of a flower. Her expansion is the tunnel to the great mystery. The vortex created in the union of these two polarities takes the pair deep into a state of ecstatic bliss and expansion where they get to bask in the rich abundance of God's love and infinitude. He holds her safe while she guides them both to God, to the truth of themselves, which is beyond ego: the realization of oneness and supreme love.

This is the true teaching of tantra, the practice of uniting energies for the purpose of experiencing higher states of consciousness. Tantra has been misrepresented to the masses, as have most sacred practices. It has been portrayed to be about superficial sexuality, concerned with mortal pleasures, when it is actually the practice of managing and conducting energy. It is a path to glimpse the sacred. Tantra is a beautiful honoring of the divine in two uniting into oneness. As we have discussed earlier, all is energy, and managing the combination of two sacred energies into an experience of one is often an experience of divine union. It can feel like meeting God, like birthing heaven on Earth.

epilogue

From the perspective of the entire universe, thank you for being willing to heal yourself. Thank you for seeking the kingdom of God first, for finding the beautiful, loving world within you, and then getting ready for all else to be added. The healing path is not just a path of self-soothing, short term "fixing" of issues. Healing is deep, long lasting, transformative, and a path to ascension. You will literally let go of lower vibrational concepts, energies, and patterning as you address the things that are keeping you from self-realization. It will feel like the hardest work you ever have done. It will feel lonely and even scary. For me, the Bible psalm "Lo I walk through the shadow of death, I shall fear no evil for thou art with me," has been my crutch in the hardest of times. The death is the falseness, the division, the lies, falling away. God is waiting where love shines brightest.

The formula of "dive deep, vibe high, radiate love" has been my guiding force for almost a decade now. This formula is concise and effective and has helped me "eloveate" to a better version of myself, enabling me to live a more authentic, satisfying life. I wish the same for you and invite you to become a part of eloveation nation, where you will find support along your journey. Boiled down to that one word, "eloveate," it is the main mission of our souls, the mission we are charged with as we incarnate.

acknowledgments

Thank you to the friends who helped with the creation of this book, you'll know who you are and how you've been a link in the production of this little book that came to me while sitting in tears, on a plane, leaving Grand Cayman, with rainbows all around. The serendipitous steps that led to discovered treasure have marked this path with people and points from Australia to the Cayman Islands, Colorado to Hatteras to my own hometown, so I thank God for divine timing and sacred spaces. My true loved ones have given me time to be quiet and receptive and to allow this to finally come to print after years of holding back. They have loved me through unusual circumstances and trusted me to follow my knowing, which gave me confidence to share what is inside me.

I learned from my three wonderful daughters and our fast world of social media to trust the value of concise, direct words. Good information doesn't always live inside lengthy, complex writing. I also thank each of my daughters for loving me as I am, with all my weirdness and for supporting me in sharing this book with you.

I thank God, most of all, because this little book came through me, not from me, from the wise mind of cosmic consciousness.

about the cover photo

This image is called "Incandescent" by Hannah Prewitt, an ocean photographer based in Australia. She loves to photograph the water because the ocean is the place where she goes to escape. Through her images, she aims to bring a sense of peace and harmony to the viewer, helping them to escape their world for a moment and feel the healing powers of the ocean as if they were in it themselves.

To learn more and see Hannah's gorgeous work, please search her on social media and find her at:

www.hannahprewitt.com

hello@hannahprewitt.com

(+61) 459 196 721

about the author

Nicole Miles lives in Eastern Pennsylvania, in the rolling hills of the Lehigh Valley. She is a lover of words, ideas, and expansion. Nicole has devoted most of her grown life to healing and self-discovery through exploring spiritual methods ranging from Ashtanga yoga, Reiki, shamanic healing, inner child work, Akashic healing, Ho' Oponopono, crystal resonance healing, forms of meditation, Ayurveda, and the list goes on. Each one is a tool to the unearthing of the truth of what she found at the core, which is LOVE.

Nicole loves being the mother of her three teenage daughters, and she loves spending time in nature and allowing herself to drift into the creative realm of spirit. Deeply empathic and intuitive, she has experienced countless moments of clear knowing, directly from the Divine, things she cannot otherwise explain how she knows or why she feels what she feels. This ability to clearly channel outside the linear mind helps her bring soothing and clarity to clients as a soul coach. She has the strong ability to see potentials and blockages for people in body, mind, and spirit.

Her work is, like this book, clear, concise, and direct, wrapped in motherly love and compassion.

Find more from Nicole at

www.eloveationnation.com

Facebook @eLOVEationnation

Instagram @eLOVEation_nation

coming soon

Nicole connected with Hannah via this exact cover photo. Like Hannah, Nicole's true sense of home is beside the ocean. When "Incandescent" was posted on Instagram, Nicole could immediately sense the elements in it—the silky feel, movement, and temperature of the water, the warmth of the generous sun saturating both the air and the water, the soothing tone of the light Hannah captured in both the water and the space above. Nicole felt this image encompassing what she knew to be the healing path, the sacred union of elements. This set in motion a great coherence of two creative souls. Please be sure to look out for the gorgeous book they will release in the very near future, combining their abilities to transport the viewer with Hannah's photography and Nicole's concentrated affirmations. It will be a book to help you, with a flip of a page, easily tap into your *inner sanctuary*.